Authentic Tales of Seven Women: The Truth of Who I Am

Edited and Co-Authored by

Demetria Hill Cannady, PhD, LPC

A Work In Progress, LLC
Valdosta, Georgia

Authentic Tales of A Woman: The Truth of Who I Am
Copyright © 2017 by Demetria Hill Cannady, PhD, LPC
All Rights Reserved

Published by:

A Work In Progress, LLC
Valdosta, Georgia 31601
(478) 227-7299
www.dhcann.09@gmail.com

ISBN-13 978-0692936160
ISBN-10 0692936165

Cover Photo Credit: Jamon Williams Photography
Final Editing Credit: Nicole Cooper, M.S. Ed, B.S. Ed

Printed in the United States of America

TABLE OF CONTENTS

Foreward   5
Ilonda Clayton, AA

Introduction   6
Demetria Hill Cannady, PhD, LPC

Additional Terms   9
Demetria Hill Cannady, PhD, LPC

Transformation   11
Demetria Hill Cannady, PhD, LPC

Brief History of Religion   30
Demetria Hill Cannady, PhD, LPC

The Journey of the Saddest Child   33
Ilonda Clayton, AA

Spiritual Crisis   45
Demetria Hill Cannady, PhD, LPC

Depression   46
Demetria Hill Cannady, PhD, LPC

For I Shall Not Die, but LIVE!   49
Tanyala Calloway

Postpartum Depression   63
Demetria Hill Cannady, PhD, LPC

Slay Your Inner Critic   67
Gena Golden, CHT, LCSW

What You Need to Know About Hypnotherapy   86
Gena Golden, CHT, LCSW

TABLE OF CONTENTS CONT.

Anxiety Disorder — 95
Demetria Hill Cannady, PhD, LPC

My Personal Quest for Bible Truth — 99
Wanda M. Thomas

The Ministries of Helps — 113
Demetria Hill Cannady, PhD, LPC

Post-Traumatic Stress Disorder — 116
Demetria Hill Cannady, PhD, LPC

You Can't Heal What You Don't Reveal — 119
Tonya Davis-Taylor, LMSW, FDLC

Self- Esteem — 127
Demetria Hill Cannady, PhD, LPC

The Steps of a P.K. (Preacher's Kid) As her World Turns — 133
Dr. Elaine Spencer Lewis

Methodology of Christian Counseling — 145
Dr. Elaine Spencer Lewis

Closing — 164
Demetria Hill Cannady, PhD, LPC

Foreword

Ilonda Clayton, AA

Women are powerful and amazing human beings. Women are driven, can multi-task, are filled with emotions, nurturing, strong, and expressive. The emotions that a woman may experience in one day is able to bring about an unfolding that only another woman is capable of understanding. Dr. Hill Cannady has assembled women from a variety of backgrounds to express their views on their spiritual journey and has it has affected their lives. These are amazing stories that show their spirit of how God used each one of us as teachers for other African American women. This book will make you smile, cry, encourage, and fill you with inspiration. It takes a brave person to share their truth. There is so much freedom in releasing your truth and seems the price you must pay to truly live a life of purpose. Understand this was not a painless process and the willingness of each person to write and share their story with such bravery.

Wayne Dyer stated, "If you change the way you look at things, the things you look at will change." How we see the world is how the world will unfold for us. I see each story in this book as a beautiful art piece. Yes! I see life as art. We all view situations, relationships, and even our relationship(s) with the creator differently. These women have open their hearts and life to the world. May you see love in every word written. May this book evoke thought and may it create a new level of compassion and awareness of the struggles that African American women go through each day just to have a voice. Only to lead you to a greater unfolding.

Introduction

Demetria Hill Cannady, PhD, LPC

My journey as a helper began in my early years as I tried to understand alcoholism and addictions. While starting in college as a business major, things just didn't feel right. In addition, I was failing all my business classes due to my genuine lack of disinterest in what the professors were talking about. I took classes from several majors (Psychology, Education, and Social Work) to see which direction I would proceed. After realizing that I didn't want to teach children for eight hours a day that ruled out being an education major. I also realized that I didn't want to "pick" people's brains all day even though Psychology was very interesting. I went to my first intern at a Day Program for people with Addictions, and fell in love with the work. I wanted to learn why people chose to abuse alcohol and drugs while it caused them and so many others so much pain, thus destroying many families including mine.

I wanted to journey into how a person became addicted, stayed addicted, recovered, relapsed, and those who stayed clean and sober for years never returning to another drink or use of any type of drugs. The stories which I've listened to over the years from all walks of line often shared the same "storyline" schemes: abandonment, abuse (all forms), molestation, and the "masking" of pain from these incidents. In listening to some of the stories, I felt myself in their shoes. I'd found my passion and became a social worker so that I could help people. I graduated with a Bachelor's in Social Work and was ready to save the world or so I thought.

The ladies who are contributors to this book will share their spiritual journey. These ladies are female ministers, prophetesses, first ladies, therapists, counselors, and life coaches. These positions fall under the realm of the "helping field." Throughout the book as you journey with everyone, you will also learn about various mental health topics and how religion and spirituality may have impacted them and/or the population they serve.

There is a difference between religion and spirituality. What is religion? Religion is defined by Merriam-Webster Dictionary as the source of worship of God or the Supernatural; commitment or devotion to religious faith or observance; a personal set or institutionalized system of religious attitudes, beliefs, and practices; scrupulous conformity; a cause, principle, or system of beliefs held to and with ardor and faith (www.merriam-webster.com).

How is spirituality defined? Merriam-Webster Dictionary defines spirituality as something that in ecclesiastical law belongs to the church or to a cleric; clergy; sensitivity or attachment to religious values; the quality or state of being spiritual. The University of Maryland Medical Center stated, "Spirituality has been defined in numerous ways, including a belief in a power operating in the universe that is greater than oneself, a sense of interconnectedness with all living creatures, and an awareness of the purpose and meaning of life and the development of personal values. It is the way you find meaning hope, comfort, and inner peace in your life. Although spirituality is often associated with religion, personal spirituality can be developed through music, art, or a connection with nature. People also find spirituality through acts of compassion and selflessness, altruism, and the experience of inner peace."

What does spirituality mean to you? Is it your personal relationship with God or your Higher Power? Is it belonging to and participating in organized religion? Does your spirituality involve you attending church, synagogue, mosque, the Kingdom Hall or the Temple? Are you an

Agnostic or an Atheist because of your lack of spirituality? Is it your prayers, silent and spoken, to God or your Higher Power? Does spirituality involve you praying, meditating, reflecting on the good of God, and/or praising and worshiping? Does spirituality give you faith, and hope? Can spirituality assist you with forgiveness of self and others? We as human may have many questions as it relates to spirituality and religion. However, we must possess a personal relationship with God or a Higher Power to grasp the concepts of religion and spirituality.

Spiritual practices improve coping skills through use of inspirational words, messages, and people; sitting still, having quiet time, meditating, or praying; music and art; and through sharing your testimony and/or life's journey. Spiritual practices allow you to help release control, gives meaning to life, gives you a better perspective on what you should be doing (passion), and your purpose. Spiritual practices offer social support, optimism and hope, reduces feelings of depression and anxiety, and encourages relaxation.

Additional Terms

Faith – an allegiance to duty or a person; fidelity to one's promises; sincerity of intentions; belief and trust in and loyalty to God; belief in traditional doctrines of a religion; something that is believed especially with strong conviction; a system of religious beliefs.

Forgiveness- the act of forgiving; forgive- to give up resentment of or claim to requital for; to grant relief from payment of; to cease of feel resentment against (an offender.

Higher Power- a spirit or being (such as God) that has a great power, strength, knowledge, etc. and that can affect nature and live the lives of people.

Hope- to cherish a desire with anticipation; to want something to happen to be true; to expect with confidence; trust.

Intercession- the act of interceding; prayer, petition or entreaty in favor of another.

Praise- to express a favorable judgment of; to glorify (a god or saint) especially by the attribution of perfections.

Worship- reverence offered a divine being or supernatural power; an act of expressing such reverence; a form of religious practice with its creed and ritual; extravagant respect or admiration for or devotion to an object of esteem.

All definitions courtesy of www.Merriam-Webster.com.

Demetria Hill Cannady, PhD, LPC, is the CEO of "A Work In Progress, LLC" a private practice in Valdosta, Georgia which focuses on Mental Health Wellness and Empowerment. She is a Licensed Professional Counselor and a Master Addictions Counselor in Georgia who counsels men, women, and children in the areas of mental health, substance abuse, behavior modification, trauma, and premarital/marriage counseling. Demetria is an Empowerment Coach who focuses on a variety of women's issues such as: self-esteem/ self-worth; relationships; single parent/blended families and family issues. Most issues can be resolved through coaching and/or counseling but requires communication; problem-solving; and goal setting.

Demetria Hill Cannady is a Certified Life Coach from the Life Coach Institute in Pensacola, Florida. She received her Bachelor's Degree in Social Work and her Master's Degree in Mental Health Counseling from Fort Valley State University in Fort Valley, Georgia. Demetria holds a PhD in Human Services with a Specialization in Counseling Studies from Capella University in Minneapolis, Minnesota. She also holds Post-Certification in Contemporary Theory in Addictive Behavior and College Teaching; both obtained through Capella University in Minneapolis, Minnesota. Demetria is a Master Addictions Counselor and is facilitator for the "Prepare Enrich" which is a Premarital/ Marriage Curriculum which focuses on enhancing new marriages and/ or repairing broken marriages. Demetria Hill Cannady is married to Garry Cannady with a blended family of three adult daughters (one of which is a newly enlisted member of the Air Force) and two biological sons together. In her spare time, she enjoys helping others to set goals, create vision boards, crochet, and playing Candy Crush.

Contact Info:

(478)227-7299
www.DemetriaHillCannady.org
Dhcann.09@gmail.com

TRANSFORMATION

DEMETRIA HILL CANNADY, PhD, LPC

My religious journey begins at the age of nine years old where I was a member of New Hope Baptist Church in Boston, Georgia. I recall being at church with my cousins, and we all made the decision to get baptized. I'm unsure if I really understood what I was doing when I made the decision, but my cousins were getting baptized, and so was I. I remember going to church on second and fourth Sundays, not really learning anything, but I was happy because I got to spend time with my cousins. We attended New Hope for at least a year or two before my mother began a "Bible" study with Jehovah's Witnesses. I remember Brother Rice coming to our home faithfully every week for "Bible" study. I remember having an attitude because it interfered with my television and telephone time. I remember going to "Book" study on Monday nights where a small group would gather to study one of the books which was assigned by the organization (Jehovah's Witness) for us to learn from. If that wasn't enough, we would go to the Kingdom Hall on Thursday nights for additional learning, and they would have "talks" on the Theocratic School (practicing how to share the "Good News" with the individuals they encountered, having Bible studies, and engaging in the door-to-door ministry). Every Sunday, we went to the Kingdom Hall where an Elder would give a "talk" (like a sermon) followed by discussion of the Watch Tower lesson for the week. As I write, I realize we were actively involved with the Kingdom Hall/ Jehovah's Witnesses. I can't say that I was spiritual because I resented being called a Jehovah's Witnesses even though everyone knew my mom was a Jehovah's Witness. I can say that I learned a lot about the Bible through the years of attending the Kingdom Hall even though I did not want to be identified as a Jehovah's Witness.

I do not recall the exact year that my mother was baptized as a Jehovah's Witness but I know that I was in middle school. I was happy for her because she was happy even though I was not happy about her becoming a Jehovah's Witness. Simply because in my mind all the "fun stuff" was being taken away. No more celebrating holidays and a boring religion (in my mind). I was a child; I didn't care anything about holidays being pagan holidays; all I know is that I wanted to celebrate them because that's what we'd always done. For some reason, two Christmases stand out in my mind. The first was when I was in the fifth grade, and I wanted to put up a Christmas tree. My mom said that we would not be putting up a tree anymore. She went on to explain that Christmas was a Pagan holiday, and we would not be participating in any more Pagan holidays. I wasn't hearing that; I went to the edge of the woods and chopped down a small pine tree. Took it back to the house, got a large flower pot (may have been a five-gallon bucket), filled it with dirt, and put my Christmas tree in it, and began decorating it with construction paper ornaments. My tree resembled "Charlie Brown's" Christmas Tree, but I didn't care because all that mattered was that I had a tree. The second memory which stands out is when I was in the seventh grade. My mom didn't celebrated Christmas, but she tolerated me celebrating it to the extent that I did: gift exchange with my friends, and gifts from my biological dad and his family. In seventh grade, my best friend gave me a pink elephant bank with green flowers painted on it. Very sentimental because I still have this bank which continues to sit on my dresser in my bedroom. I think this year stands out because someone told me that I was a Jehovah's Witness, and I shouldn't be celebrating Christmas, or maybe it's because I still have this bank. I don't know if I was hurt or angry because I was being called a Jehovah's Witness. In my mind, "How dare they call me a Jehovah's Witness. I haven't been baptized as a Jehovah's Witness. I was baptized as a Baptist and I'm still a Baptist." As children, our minds work in mysterious ways.

While I learned a lot about the Bible throughout my years of attending the Kingdom Hall, I didn't want to be seen or known for knocking on people's doors (while they hide from me) trying to share the Bible with them, especially people that I did not know. In addition, I was a very shy child and hated to speak in public.

When my mother started her study with the Jehovah's Witnesses she was married to her second husband, and he was all but a "good guy." He had an extensive list of flaws with the most important being that he was an addict, and I did not like him. Brother Rice tried his hardest to support and keep my mother's husband in line with biblical principles, but he wasn't successful. However, the Jehovah's Witnesses were very supportive to my mother and myself; they made sure we had when no one else did. My mother's husband ended up going to jail and while he was incarcerated, she filed and was granted a divorce.

I attended the Kingdom Hall with my mother until I graduated from high school and went to college. I went to college in 1991, and the entire six years that I was in college (undergraduate and graduate), I never attended church for worship services. I attended the Kingdom Hall once or twice while in college, but that was it. I only attended church once which was when I was being initiated into Alpha Kappa Alpha Sorority Inc. I went home once a month while in college and would attend the Kingdom Hall during my home visits. Other than that, I went for years with no religion and very little spirituality. I did not engage in any religious or political conversations, this was my policy, and I stuck to it for years.

While attending graduate school in 1997, I became pregnant with my first child. It was not a planned pregnancy, and to be honest, I didn't really know or like the guy from whom I was pregnant (a rebound relationship). We had only been dating for a few months and had unprotected sex which resulted in an unplanned pregnancy. I was not happy about being pregnant, having an abortion wasn't an option, and being pregnant was the consequences of my unprotected actions. Even though I was twenty-three years old, I felt like I wasn't ready for a baby, especially from a man with whom I wasn't in love. Being pregnant and unmarried went against the religious grain, so I don't think it would have mattered with which religion I was affiliated. My mom was due to get married in April 1997 to her third husband, so I hid the fact that I was pregnant until she returned from her honeymoon. I found out in February and didn't tell my mom and stepdad until late April. My mom was angry, my biological dad was absent, and my stepdad wouldn't talk to me. They eventually got over me being pregnant, came around, and started back talking to me.

In 1998, after numerous deaths on the maternal side of my family, not knowing much about the daycares in the middle Georgia area, and my daughter's father stating that he was moving to Florida, I made the decision to move back home to Boston, GA to have some help from my family with my daughter. My parents were supposed to be moved out of my mother's house and into my stepfather's house by the time I moved back to Boston which is where I would be living. This didn't happen; they stayed in my mother's house another two years along with my daughter and me. Since they were still in the home, I felt obligated to attend the Kingdom Hall every Sunday.

I knew that I didn't want to be a Jehovah's Witness, but I lived with them, and I felt guilty lying in bed on Sundays when they were getting dressed to go to the Kingdom Hall. Eventually, my parents moved into my step dad's house, and I stopped attending the Kingdom Hall because I no longer felt obligated to go. While I learned a lot, I felt that the religion itself was too stringent for me. I felt uptight just thinking about trying to uphold the biblical principles/standards associated with being a Jehovah's Witness. "Walking that very straight and very narrow line." At this point, I only attended the Kingdom Hall sporadically and attended church when there was a family event (paternal side) such as a family reunion, and everyone else was going.

Fast forward a few years, I moved to Valdosta, GA in 2007 while pregnant with my second child; different father and still unmarried. Oh yeah, I was "shacking" too. I was in a relationship with a man, Garry Cannady, that I loved and we'd been together for a few years, but we were shacking and having a child out of wedlock. He'd proposed to me a year or two before I got pregnant, but I didn't want to get married. I was making my decision based upon the views of my mother who was on her third marriage, and I didn't want any parts of marriage. I had no problems with shacking, but my significant other did. During this period, I still wasn't attending church or practicing any religious beliefs. I said my routine prayers every night, but I was just existing. It was when I had my third child, still unmarried almost three years later when some things begin to change. July 2007, I became employed with Valdosta Technical College as an Adult Education Instructor (GED), and I met a woman by the name of Kelisa Brown who was the staff member who trained me how to conduct the orientation for individuals who were pursuing a GED. We became friends from there, not sure how but we did. Kelisa was "saved;" and I'd never had a "saved" friend before. This was a new experience.

Kelisa would often talk to me about God, going to church, and how getting "saved" saved her life. She would invite myself and my family to go to church with her. Kelisa would constantly talk to me about God, about spirituality, developing a relationship with God, and about finding a good church home. My reply to her would often be, "Just keep me in prayer." She never gave up on me though; she was persistent for many years! Kelisa always displayed a sincere Christian attitude, believed in her biblical principles, and stood up for her spirituality and religious beliefs. My pattern, on the other hand, continued, "Just keep me in prayer. Keep me on the prayer list", and she continued praying for myself and my family.

In 2014, things changed for me; after six years of hearing Kelisa say that I needed to increase my prayer life, increase my faith, and find a church home, it began to sink in. 2014 started off a bit "rocky;" I started "A Work In Progress, LLC," counseling agency, had several altercations which were two steps short of physical violence, so I decided to take Kelisa up on her advice with trying to get my spiritual life in order. She said, "I guarantee you put God in it, everything else will fall into place." I started visiting churches within the area in attempts to find a church home. She visited a few churches with me, one church we visited left us both confused after hearing the sermon. My question, "I know I haven't been in church in a while but did I miss something?" She replied, "I think we both missed something." This was not good since she was saved and knew the word. Result, this was not the place I needed to be.

The next church I visited was in Quitman, Church of Perfecting Saints, which I'd visited before on a few occasions with my husband. This visit was with my husband and children on Mother's Day 2014. Every time that I'd visited this church in the past, it was warm, inviting, and

I left understanding the message presented. There was no "yelling or screaming"; this allowed me to process what was being taught. I left feeling good because I understood the "word" and my spirit was at ease. I didn't feel uptight or uneasy while sitting in church. I attended Church of Perfecting Saints the next Sunday and every Sunday following the first Sunday, except for one Sunday that I was sick and fifth Sundays (due to no church). My family and I attended the church for two years before becoming members. Some of the church members thought that we were already members because we were actively working in the church.

My thought process is that God was preparing me for the tsunami that was about to enter my life by getting me spiritually rooted and planted in a church home. The tsunami hit in June 2014. My world and my business that I began building in January was crumbling right in front of me, and I couldn't get clear answers. Everything was spiraling before me, and I had no control. The business that I thought was prosperous even though delayed with payments plummeted in the blink of an eye. In my trying to take a shortcut to get my business started, I entered a verbal contract with a Licensed Professional Counselor (LPC) to subcontract with her agency; I would provide the services to the children, and she would bill them under her provider number at a percentage since I still wasn't fully licensed. My team and I started seeing children in February so we were anticipating reimbursements from February to at least May. The LPC assured me that we would receive monies in sixty days' maximum so we anticipated having monies by April at latest. After months of anticipation of reimbursements and denials of reimbursements, the billing clerk informed me that the LPC was credentialed as an individual but not as an agency. Since she was not credentialed as an agency, that equated to no reimbursement for services which had been provided by myself and my staff over the past few months. It would be an additional three to six months before she would be properly credentialed. However, the LPC wasn't relaying this information to me, her billing clerk was. At this point, she had yet to call and notify me that there were any problems. The LPC would not answer any of my calls nor was she returning my calls. My thought process: "I have staff to pay; I have an office space to pay for; My bills are behind; What the hell? There is no money coming. What am I supposed to do next?" Shocked would be an understatement. Hurt, disappointment, anger, and shame was what I began to feel daily following the news that there would be no money to pay for any services that we'd provided the past few months. Every morning after learning this information, I would wake up, and I would sit on my sofa and stew in self-pity. This lasted for about two months. The only time that I would go outside my home was on Sundays. On Sundays, I would put on my "mask," go to church, praise the Lord, come home, cook dinner, and go back to sitting on my sofa.

Kelisa continued to emphasize to pray for guidance and let God lead me. I didn't know what that meant- "Let God lead me." I had always taken charge of my situations and my life. This was the first time that I truly felt helpless. I had no control and didn't know where to begin to pick the pieces up, let alone how to put them back together. In addition to not being able to get paid for the work, my husband and I found out the house that we were renting and had been living in for the past six years was being auctioned off the following week because it was up for foreclosure. We did not find out through our landlord; we found out due to people coming by to look at the house because they were interested in purchasing it at the auction. One of the men who came by to look at the house asked us, if he purchased the house, would we agree to continue living in it. We agreed to stay; we didn't have any money to go anywhere else, nor did we have anywhere to go. The new landlord allowing us to remain in the home was one of God's blessings! The house was auctioned off the following week, and the guy purchased the house and came by afterwards to confirm his purchase. To add additional frustration to the current situation, my vehicle was repossessed in the middle of the night. The auto finance company changed without my knowledge, and I was thirty days past due with the old finance company, but the new finance company was showing ninety days past due. No warning- vehicle was just gone. I felt hopeless, but I had faith that things would work out for me. I had nothing but faith now and it was a bit bleak.

I didn't have a job because I was building my business and my husband had been laid off as well. I had one child that I was seeing through another agency twice a week for one hour as a favor for a friend. How was I going to pay a bill with that? Let alone pay staff which had been working for me the past few months. What was I going to do with these children whom I had been providing therapeutic services? Was I going to refer them to another agency? Would I be discharging them from services? Would I try to subcontract with another agency? A bunch of questions for which I had no answers.

At this stage, I decided to sit still and listen for a sign, a word, a message, something from God. I needed instructions and guidance on what to do next. I had been hearing about "faith" so I decided to put this "faith thing" into practice. I was already praying but was unsure if I was praying correctly, so I was trying to develop an appropriate strategy for my situation and new-found spirituality. I began contacting other agencies to subcontract with them, I was unsuccessful. One agency just wanted the children and didn't offer me employment. I felt somewhat defeated. I transferred services of the kids to the agency that I was contracting with for the one child. They allowed me to come to their office and work within the office, as well as, continue to allow me to see the children that I was working with through my agency. There was a significant difference in pay as I would only be making one-third of what I would be making if I were billing them for myself. Nevertheless, it was income, so I was appreciative. It was not full-time employment, but this job allowed me to pay those individuals who worked with me and allowed me to pay some bills.

Mid-July 2014, I decided to come out of my pity party and take charge of my life. I got on my computer and applied for full licensure; securing the necessary documents, signatures, and paying the application fee. There was a glitch with my clinical hours, so my application didn't get processed in August 2014. I took another route, got the signature needed for my clinical hours, and was granted full licensure in September 2014. Praise God. I applied for a Medicaid Provider number in October 2014, which at the time was a paper or computer application process. I completed the paper application which would take forty-five days versus thirty days (computer application) to get an answer. I received a Medicaid Provider number in December 2014 which allowed me to apply to become a behavioral health provider through insurance panels.

In October 2014, I was asked to participate in a radio show to discuss the topic of parenting. I was excited as I had never done radio before. Because of my participation in the radio show, a few months later, I became involved with a group, I AM ME University, where I met some lovely ladies. At this point, I was still trying to figure things out in areas of my life as were most of the women in the group. This group hosted prayer calls on Tuesday evenings; I never missed the prayer calls because the messages were good, and I needed all the prayer I could get. There were two individuals that would lead these prayer calls, and then there was one individual who was an intercessor (at the time I didn't really know what that meant or what that consisted of) in the group for the calls. I didn't trust everyone to pray for me, but it was something about Prophetess Shalonda Williams and Minister Raleigh Thornton that allowed me to allow them to pray for me and I received it. It was probably because they were transparent and displayed their human side and how God changed them during their mess. I was dedicated to the Tuesday night prayer calls. The Tuesday night prayer calls eventually ended because Prophetess Shalonda had her own prayer calls on Wednesday nights, and Minister Raleigh was about to start ministry school.

No one prepared me for the rollercoaster of the journey which I would take in changing my life spiritually. Who knew that there would be so many attacks from the enemy by attempting to live right, uphold biblical principles, and avoid obstacles around every corner. Trying to get approved behavioral health provider with insurance panels was another roller coaster ride and prayer was the only thing that "kept me" while in the waiting phase. The process which I assumed would take thirty to sixty days took six to nine months. I received approval from Aetna and Blue Cross Blue Shield in January 2015 and Cenpatico (Peach State) in June 2015. Amerigroup had staff changes to occur during my credentialing phase, so I had to complete my application over again because the previous application didn't get processed during nor after staff changes. All I kept saying to myself was, "Patience is a virtue." I had very little patience, and to me, this was my learning lesson in patience.

August 2015, I started to participate is a spiritual challenge titled "A Closer Walk," conducted by Prophetess Shalonda Williams. It consisted of thirty days of getting closer to God with studying types of prayers, various scriptures, the topic of intercession, watching videos of sermons from various pastors, gospels passages, tackled forgiveness, and the such. Within this study, I learned there are a variety of prayers, how to pray and intercede on behalf of others, and I learned how to forgive. The one area that I thought forgiveness was impossible occurred because of participating in the "A Closer Walk Challenge" (the second time I participated in the challenge). I participated in the "A Closer Walk Challenge" four times, and I only completed all thirty days once. Each time I participated, it seemed like all hell would break loose inside and outside my family unit with the direct targets being my daughter or my husband. I know now these were distractions for me, so I would become consumed with my family and not complete the challenge.

Along this journey, there were some prophecies given to me. I'd always been hesitant when people stated that they received a prophetic word. My question would be, "How did you know this message came from God and not someone pretending to receive a word from God?" The first time I received a prophetic word, I was on the telephone, and I was glad because I was looking crazy and saying, "Yeah right! Me in real estate? Compassion for people and their homeless situation, yes, but real estate?" I laughed for a while! A few months later, I received an invitation to attend a seminar regarding real estate and buying properties. I laughed again and said it's coincidence! Over the years, there have been some additional prophetic messages, and most have come to fruition, in part or into full fruition. I no longer doubt prophetic words, but it also depends on the messenger.

An additional business test: The woman who was the billing clerk for the LPC which I attempted to subcontract with shared with me that when I became an approved Medicaid/ Behavioral Health Provider with insurance panels, she would assist me with submitting my billing and getting reimbursement for services. After I got approval from the insurance panels, I contacted the billing clerk to let her know that I was an approved provider from insurance panels. She immediately began to put the components in place so that I could begin getting paid for the consumers with whom I was providing services. All paperwork was in order and ready for her to begin billing, then she had surgery. After her surgery, in November 2015, she attempted to get the ball rolling again with my billing and reimbursements, but the physician to whom she'd been providing billing services for years had two grandchildren to die. The billing clerk stated that she had too much going on and would not be able to do my billing for me. She said that she would to forward me all the passwords and walk me through doing the billing for myself. After this conversation, I didn't hear any more from her. She wouldn't answer her phone or return my emails. I was locked out of all my stuff needed to bill for services. I had an office in Thomasville, GA, was seeing children, and not receiving reimbursement because my billing person was MIA. Again, I was stuck because I was depending on someone else to handle my business!

Well, I contacted the necessary people (Insurance panels, clearinghouses, etc.) to reclaim all my accounts by verifying my identity, changing passwords, faxing forms and identification confirming that I was who I said that I was. It took about thirty days to get everything transferred back to my name as the account administrator. Here I was again with no billing person and no knowledge on how to complete the billing to get reimbursed for the services which I'd been providing.

A new year (2016) rolls in and I had reclaimed my business identity for billing purposes, but I still didn't know how to bill for services nor had I secured a person to complete the billing.

In March 2016, I moved into an office space in Valdosta, GA which was one of my goals. My office was within a local church, but I was providing services in an office setting (again) versus going into the home setting. Also in March, I swallowed my pride and asked a woman that I knew was familiar with billing if she would be interested in billing for me. I had some "negative vibes" about her doing my billing, but I felt desperate and I was tired of seeing children with no reimbursements. All the families thought I was getting paid for seeing their children when in fact I was not. I agreed to provide services to their children and that was all they needed to know. Out of desperation, a verbal agreement was made with the new billing clerk, and in May 2016, I received my first reimbursement check from an insurance provider. The months prior to receiving any reimbursements for services, I continued to work in Tifton with my part-time job, have vision board parties, do consultations, complete policy and procedure manuals, life coaching sessions, DNA testing, and home studies to ensure that I had money to cover my household. My hustle and my faith was strong. I was determined to be successful and make my business work with working hard, countless prayers, faith, persistence, and the support from my family. My husband was paying most the bills, so I could actively work on my business by putting the money I made back into the business. Entrepreneurship was by far one of the hardest things outside of parenting and marriage that I'd ever done in my life!

Things took a drastic turn in April 2016. We were doing "ok" financially -getting the bills paid, sustaining my business, and making a small profit. My family and I were headed to church one Sunday morning and my husband, Garry, received a call from our Pastor. They had a conversation about him becoming an ordained deacon within the church. Garry was told to discuss it with me and let the Pastor know after church what his decision would be. My thought was,

"You're already doing the work of a deacon so why not." After church, Garry accepted the invitation to become ordained as a deacon. Later that Sunday evening, he received a call from his employer to inform him that his services were no longer needed with their company. Who does that? Who terminates someone on a Sunday evening? He thanked them for employment for the past year and wished them well. About thirty minutes later, his employer's mother called and told him that he needed to be at work Monday morning because her son didn't have the authority to terminate anyone. My husband shared with her that her son terminated him, and he would not be returning to work, but he would be there in the morning to collect his belongings and his tools.

Garry accepted the invitation to be ordained as a deacon that morning and was terminated that night. He had been praying to God for the past few months about wanting to work with children. Technically, he asked God to remove him from this job even though he did not anticipate it happening in this way nor at the time it happened. I reminded him of what he'd prayed for and shared with him to use this opportunity to do something different - help me build the business. I work with kids, he wanted to work with kids; it seemed like a perfect match to me! My husband began assisting me in working with the children in May 2016; the children enjoyed him, and he appeared to enjoy being with the children. He appeared to have some peace being away from the old job but missed working with the heavy equipment and having a paper check in hand.

I wasn't physically attending Bible Study, just church on Sundays. However, I got on Prophetess Shalonda's prayer calls every Wednesday night to get my "Bible study." I took notes on these calls, wrote down the scriptures, read them, and applied them to what I was learning from church as well. Her messages and my pastor's messages reflected and paralleled each other almost weekly. In addition to that, Prophetess Shalonda prophesied during this period that I would go into ministry, not pulpit ministry and that my husband would totally surrender to God giving him unspeakable joy. I laughed at the thought of me in ministry. I have a bad habit called profanity so me and ministry didn't seem to match, but who was I to say what God wasn't going to do with me.

May or June of 2016, we started to attend Bible study at church; one of the best decisions ever. After Bible study, I would get on the prayer calls with Prophetess Shalonda and listen in until the message ended. We started conversing after church with various individuals, and I eventually stopped calling in for the prayer calls. I missed Shalonda's prayer calls but would get on the calls on the Wednesdays that we didn't have Bible study. Fall 2016, a situation arose with a young girl of whom I was an acquaintance, and I was approached about mentoring young girls. My response was that I felt like I need to start with the parents and women first and then work my way to the younger girls. Part of my focus has always been toward the African American women population. I spoke with the Co-Pastor regarding monthly sessions with the teenage girls/women at the church and she agreed. I also spoke with Pastor for clearance as well- he thought it to be an awesome idea.

I laughed to myself because Prophetess Shalonda had prophesied earlier that I would be in the ministry but not pulpit ministry. It appeared that I was about to have a women's ministry addressing self-help and mental health topics within the church. I was hesitant to get started because I didn't want anyone feeling that I was trying to run things and/or take over at the church. A meeting was held with the Co-Pastor and another church member to collaborate with the fellowship which was already in place. The meeting went well, and we all agreed that the new year would be an appropriate time to get started. At the beginning of the year, 2017, I began to feel conflicted about having not started, so I scheduled a day and held the first "Women's Fellowship" in February 2017. I had an awesome time educating and fellowshipping, and the women in attendance stated that they had an enjoyable time being able to learn and share information about themselves while enjoying fellowship with other women.

Mid-March 2017 is when I realized that I was receiving another message from God, thus, telling me that I need to have all my business affairs, especially financial affairs, in my possession. After waiting approximately two weeks for a reimbursement check to come in and not receiving one, I reached out to my billing person to inquire as to when the last time she'd submitted billing. Her reply was that she'd submitted billing at the beginning of the month. Well I decided to go in the system and browse around myself, and I was unable to see where billing was submitted. Next, I contact a clearinghouse administrator for their assistance with learning and working my way through the system. After he finished walking me through what I needed to do and how to do it, I then asked him if the system would show the last time claims were billed. The gentleman was quiet for quite a while. I said hello to ensure that he was still on the line and he was. He stated that he wanted to make sure that he was giving me accurate information, and from what he saw the last time, claims were file on the 16th of the prior month. Shocked, upset, and angry but all I could do was to laugh to keep from crying.

Here I was in the same position again on another level; a billing person whose urgency was not my urgency. To make a long story short, I reached out for help for someone to teach me how to do the billing but was unsuccessful. I ended up teaching myself through trial and error. I was successful with some claims and with the others not so much but I was happy to receive some money versus no money. In receiving money, I learned that I could do one of the things, billing, I feared the most.

To me, this was another learning lesson as I stated; the first individual had my billing information tied up, and I could receive no reimbursements and didn't have access to my own information, the second individual for whatever reason stopped filing the claims, and the third time a billing issue arose I ended up learning how to do my own billing. "They say" third times a charm. The experience with the Licensed Counselor was the first learning lesson to not take short cuts, stay the course, and trust the process. The experiences with my business may be what God ordered for me as a starting point to get my spiritual life and my household in order. My business grew because my spiritual life grew because I finally learned the art of sitting still and seeking God's voice prior to deciding. God has a way of getting our attention, and sometimes it's not always through direct experiences.

As I reflected on numerous vision boards which I have completed in the past; counseling, life coaching, and women's groups were always at the top my vision boards. I just did not view counseling and helping people as a ministry until this past year. Counseling is a ministry, helping others is a ministry, but I had not viewed it as such until I started to regularly attend Bible Study weekly on Wednesday nights. In the most recent of months, we had Bible study on the ministries of helps. It's amazing the Aha moments that we have when we are truly paying attention. As I reflected over the past three years, my spiritual journey has been amazing. I basically went without a spiritual life for over twenty years, especially as an adult to being very spiritual in the past three years. I'm not sure how I made it so far for so long without having a spiritual life, but I can say that I am thankful for developing a spiritual and a prayer life. I can now say that I have my own intimate relationship with God. I can ask people to pray for me but I have learned how to pray for myself, my family, my friends, and the individuals which I work with. Transformation can be a lovely thing.

Brief History of Religion as It Relates to Mental Health
Demetria Hill Cannady, PhD, LPC

In researching religion and mental health the conversations dated back to 1882 with Jean Charcot linking religion with hysteria and neurosis. Sigmund Freud regarded God as an illusion which he stated was based on the facts that people felt the need to have a powerful father figure. In his book, *Obsessive Actions and Religious Practices* (1907), he suggests that religion and neurosis are comparable products of the human mind: neurosis, with its compulsive behavior, is "an individual religiosity," and religion, with its repetitive rituals, is a "universal obsessional neurosis." Freud believes humans created gods- "we know that like gods [demons] are only the product of the psychic powers of man; they have been created from and out of something (Moses and Monotheism, 1939).

The Diagnostic and Statistical Manual of Mental Disorders (DSM) which is formulated by the American Psychological Association has several editions over the course of years. Within the DSM III religion is portrayed negatively by suggesting that religious and spiritual experiences are examples of psychopathology. The DSM III-R provided unfair stereotypes of religious persons thus labeling them under Dissociative Disorder, Not Otherwise Specified. The DSM IV- Code-V62.89 includes three categories as it relates to religion: normal religion and spiritual experiences; religious and spiritual problems leading to mental disturbances; and mental disturbances with a religious and spiritual context. Within the DSM V (most current edition), there is the Diagnostic Category: Religious and Spiritual Problems which focuses attention on religious or spiritual problems such as distressing experiences that involve loss or questioning faith, problems associated with conversion to a new faith, or questioning spiritual values that may not be related to an organized church or religious institution.

Mental health has two dimensions: absence of mental illness and the presence of well-adjusted personality that contributes to the life of the community. The lack of spirituality can interfere with interpersonal relationships and can contribute to the genesis of psychiatric disturbance. Mental Health Professional such as therapist, Counselors, Psychiatrists have deemed too much and distorted religion to be associated with the mental health diagnosis of Schizophrenia. However, as helping professionals we strive to assist the individuals we serve to obtain mental wellness, emotional stability, and balance.

American Psychiatric Association (2013). Diagnostic and statistical manual of mental disorders, 5th Ed. Washington, DC.

Ilonda Clayton is founder of Open Your Heart Life Coaching, a website (ilonda_clayton.com), Instagram (therealilonda), and Twitter (shermyaclayton) which inspires the broken hearted to find healing and purpose. Open Your Heart Life Coaching was started by her search for her own healing and encouragement and lead to her wanting to share her journey to overcome obstacles. In addition, to share her gift of writing and coaching to others. Ilonda's mission is to help those to deal with Stress Management, Balance, Spirituality, Personal Growth, Motivation, Depression, Loss and Family/ Parenting through coaching, yoga, and meditation practices. Ilonda believes these tools and reconnection with what truly makes people happy on the inside. Ilonda is a Certified Child Advocate laws (court appointed), Domestic Violence after-care and procedures, Client Support Work (behavior management) in adult/ child care.

She obtained an Associate's Degree in Criminal Justice from University of Phoenix and has over 8 years' experience in mental health. She is a Certified Yoga Instructor. Ilonda has a heart to help others and truly enjoys her work. Before transitioning into coaching, Ilonda worked in various jobs as a cashier at a large retail store to a file clerk at a doctor's office, even trying her hand at opening her own clothing store. She knew these career choices did not satisfy her. Ilonda felt she had a purpose to do something that would truly fulfill her. In 2012, she made the decision to walk away from her job and go back to school full-time. She knew this was the best choice for her and although it was not easy. Ilonda has been homeless, broke, suffered from depression, and even went through a divorce all while raising three children. Ilonda understands that all these events made her stronger and even more determined than ever to share gifts with the world.

Facebook: Open Your Heart and Let Your Soul Smile
Twitter: Shermya Clayton
Instagram :therealilonda
Website: www.ilondalcayton.com

The Spiritual Journey of the Saddest Child

Ilonda Clayton, AA in Criminal Justice

As a child, I would have recurring dreams. I would be walking down a beautiful street holding hands with my mom and dad. Both smiling at me as I looked up at them, feeling so loved. Then during the dream, I would hear my mother say in the most intimidating voice; "Wake your behind up! Don't make me get my belt! Get up and clean your room! You have plenty to do around here and it'd better be done by the time I get home! "Yes Ma'am" I would say. She, my brother, and step dad would always go grocery shopping on Saturdays. "You always laying in the bed," she would say on the way down the stairs. I knew it would all have to be done by the time they returned. I never really had a lot of happy weekends as a child, and this went on until I left home at the age of 16. I can remember crying and asking God, "Why me! Why am I not pretty enough, or smart enough?" I would cry for hours.

My mother let me know that I was not the daughter she had hoped for. The fact that my father abandoned me only made matters worse. I was convinced that I was not worthy of love. From the endless beatings, the verbal abuse, the months of punishments, to the mean disapproving looks, it was years of me never feeling like I was good enough for anything but abuse. The saddest part was, we attended Bible study regularly. I always struggled with how someone could learn about God, only to be angry and hateful day after day. My sadness and vibrant imagination became my best friends. My sadness was strangely, somewhat of a comfort to me. A familiar companion that I could depend on. My imagination led me to places far away from my reality and helped me cope with the pain.

I rarely smiled as a child and although I lacked self-esteem and wore sadness like a garment, I somehow still managed to believe in God. My relationship with Him inspired hope for one who, otherwise, would have been hopeless. Through it all, I believe that my relationship with my creator brought little miracles into my life that kept me from giving up. Like, the one friend that I confided in about what was happening to me. She pleaded with me to tell someone. One day, after being beaten by a cord, I tried to convince her that it was my fault. Being the friend that she was, she wouldn't buy my explanation and after much persuading from her, I finally went to the guidance counselor. I had reached my breaking point, but still, even as I sat in front of the counselor, I tried to justify why I had been beaten. As she took pictures of my bruises, she stopped and said, "No one deserves to be beaten." I really began to open up that day and as the counselor and I talked, I realized that it wasn't just the beatings that scared me and broke my heart, but it was the way my mother treated me in general. She always knew how to make me feel like dirt and seemed to enjoy doing so.

My mother and the state worker arrived at the same time and I listened to her defending herself by saying that I was such a bad child and that she was just a caring mother trying to do her best to raise her children right. I watched this woman and heard her words, she looked and sounded like my mother, but I had never met this innocent, victim of a woman who stood before me. As the state worker was getting ready to leave, she pulled me aside and gave me her card. She told me to call her if I needed her. As much as I appreciated that, it wasn't much comfort to me. I knew things would go back to the way they were; that the innocent victim would disappear and the monster would return. I was right. My mother was so angry that I had exposed her, that she took the mental and emotional abuse to heights that I'd never imagined, even for her. Although the physical beatings stopped after that day, I knew it was time for me to leave.

A relative in Georgia agreed to let me live with them until I was ready to be on my own. I knew that moving was best for me, but there was a part of me who wished that things were different. I wished that I had the relationship with my mother like my friends had with their mothers. I wished that she loved me like the mothers on television loved their daughters. More than anything, I just wished she would have told me that she was sorry for all she had done or maybe asked me to stay.

Moving to Georgia was an eye-opening experience for me. It didn't take me long to have a better understanding of why my mother acted the way she did. Her mother was abusive too. They both are very critical of everything that I do, even to this day. It is hard for me to admit, but abusive relationships seemed to follow me into adulthood. After all, it was all I knew. This made it very hard for me as a mother. I was never taught how to love and nurture, but I was determined not to be like my mother and grandmother. The cycle would stop with me.

I am Forgiveness. I am Forgiven.

I choose not to go into every detail of abuse that I endured at the hands of people who should have protected me and out of respect for the people that have been through abuse. I want my story to be one of hope, and belief and not bitterness and unforgiveness. After many years of abuse, it all came to a head through long bouts of depression. I felt unworthy to live at times. However, I realized that things had to change. I had turned my back on religion and I honestly felt that I could not live up to the standards that was set by the church, but I remembered that relationship with God that had given me hope as an abused child, and was willing to try again.

Growing up, although we attended Bible study and Sunday service, we never prayed and going to church never seemed to change how my mom treated me. This experience really turned me off to the idea of church. I had three children out of wedlock, and because of all the mistakes I'd made in life, I wondered how God could use me. Still, I reluctantly began attending church again. To my surprise, I fell in love with everything about it. Then, when I opened up about how I felt and about some of my experiences, I never felt truly supported by the church. Instead, I felt judged and ashamed.

My depression began to get worse and even though I had gone to therapy, it hadn't help. I had gone to therapy on and off throughout the years, and eventually, I finally found a therapist that worked well for me. She showed me that my depression was a part of mourning the loss of my parents who abandoned and abused me and that my mother's issues are with herself, and not me. I attended parenting classes and participated in therapy with my children to help heal the damage that I had done to them because of not knowing how to love and nurture them. Through the grace of God, they have forgiven me. During this time, I had to break away from a lot of people who stalled and prevented my healing process. The hardest part of this life transition was forgiving myself. The guilt of every mistake would often keep me up at night. I prayed and asked God to help me and He answered by sending a special woman into my life.

I opened up and told her about my life and my decisions. She explained to me that I was only doing what I knew how to do. During our conversation, she used the metaphor of a baby being born and how a parent sees that child as innocent and nothing they could do could turn their love away. Now for someone that never felt unconditional love from a parent, it was hard for me to grasp. My reference for what constitutes love is very different than someone who had a healthy relationship with their parents. I dug deep into my imagination and visualized a mother viewing her child, and attached my name to it. I was overcome with emotion. At that moment, I realized that God loved me, no matter what! You see, I felt that religion taught me that I was a terrible person, and I was going to hell. But, I now know that God and religion are two very different things.

I had never had a revelation of how much God loved me. I began to feel my emotions and my spirit shift. At this point, I wish I could tell you that my story ended with some wonderful and happy ending but even after starting the healing process, there was still much more work to do. Thankfully, my new-found sense of being loved unconditionally had strengthened me for the task.

The Work

"The Gateway to wisdom and knowledge are always open"

Reprogramming my mind was the first and most important thing I had to do. I was told for so long that I was stupid, ignorant, sorry, and more. I had no idea how to think positively about myself or how to love myself. So, I held onto my knowledge of God's love for me. I'm so thankful that I discovered His love. Because of it, I began to believe that I could do whatever I dreamed. Still, the memories haunted me. Like the time when I was twelve years old, and my mother and stepfather called me downstairs. My grades were terrible, and I had never done anything that my mother considered to be a talent. She asked me, "What do you want to do with your life because your grades are bad and at this rate you will never do anything at all." I sat there and even after her negative comment, the child in me that craved validation, blurted out, "I want to be a movie star!" I felt happy about myself, mainly because I really said what was on my heart. My mother leaned over and laughed until she cried stating, "You? It will never happen. Go back upstairs." As I walked away, the tears rolled down my face. I could hear them laughing and saying, "She is so stupid."

Twenty-six years after that incident, my mother and I were on the phone. She said, "Do you remember when you wanted to be a movie star? I had to put some kind of reality in you." My heart sunk again. As I put down the phone, I cried every bit of pain I had ever felt in my life. I felt that overwhelming sense of sadness again. The woman that I called mother had been so broken in her life that she had no other option but to break me too. I realized that for me to change, I had to cut her out of my life completely. So, I did.

I asked God to teach me how to love me, to allow me to see myself the way He sees me. I knew that if I didn't learn to love myself, I had no chance of changing. I had heard before that words had power and knew it to be true since the words of my mother had always cut my heart like a knife. Although I had always heard the negativity from my mother, grandmother, and other family members, I knew I had to choose positivity. I still can't answer the question of "Why me?" but that's no longer even important. I had to figure out how to get to the other side of it all and go from extreme negativity to extreme positivity. I searched the Internet, read books, listened to lectures, and anything that had to do with the word love, self-love, and self-worth. Just like I had heard the negative repeatedly, I had to hear positive repeatedly. Positive books, positive television...I even listened to positive music. In the past, I loved listening to sad love songs that fed my own sadness.

I had to reprogram my mind and change all the negative talk that I taught myself to believe. In the book, "You Can Heal Your Life" by Louise L. Hay, she writes, "What we think about ourselves becomes the truth for us." It took a lot of work in therapy and being on my own to understand that what I was taught about me was not true. The ones who taught me this were damaged themselves. Today, I still must do daily work. When emotions rise about the pain of what I was and about what people said about me, I remember a time in therapy where I was asked, "What do I do when I need to cry?" I had always thought that tears meant that I was weak. My therapist helped me understand that crying helps us to release pain. I now believe that tears are our silent prayers to God.

In my life, I have experienced physical pain that seemed unbearable, but the mental pain would hit me even harder. I would fall to the ground and cry for extended periods of time, not from being hit but from the memory of the sting of words. I can now embrace the fact that it was all part of the healing process. After realizing that I was not only mourning my parent's abandonment and abuse, but also the loss of who I wanted them to be and how I wanted to be loved by them, I had to realize that what they gave me is all they had to give me. We don't get to choose how people love us, we only get to choose what we will tolerate in our lives. The hardest part was coming to terms with the fact that all forms of abuse in my life (love relationships, friends, lovers, and parents) would never stop until I learned how to set boundaries.

"No one knows enough to be a Pessimist"

The absolute truth is I will have to do daily work on myself for the rest of my life, most people do though. I lost a lot of years that I should have been getting to know myself. Instead I was looking for love in all the wrong places. Once upon a time, if drama or abuse was not involved in a relationship, I wanted no part of it because to me, that was "normal." Self-love was not an option for me, now it is a must. Even though I was learning principles of self-love, I had a tough time believing what I was learning. The abused part of me was still looking for love by doing what everyone else thought was acceptable. I thought I needed to get married because if I did what everyone else was doing, maybe that would make me happy. Boy, was I wrong! I never really sat down and thought about what I really wanted. Instead, I did what I was programmed to do.

The free spirit in me, the true me, was trying desperately to come out, but I fought against it and so my unbalanced and reckless decisions continued. Most of the time, my choices left me looking like a fool in many situations. The other part of me was a free spirit which was the true part of me that wanted to come out. I realized that I did not yet know enough about self-love to be pessimistic about it so I decided to keep learning.

"Let Go of What You Think is Supposed to Happen"

I had to open my heart to God's dream for my life and what that truly meant. I looked back into my imagination and some wisdom that was given to me by a man named Matthew I met while working in a retail store. It is amazing how God sends wisdom when you need it the most. I can remember venting to him about how I didn't really know what to do or how to be in this world. "What was my purpose?" "How do you go on after the abuse, when you have no mother or father to look up to?" The young man told me, "Just become the woman you want to be". How simple? I could be a kind, nurturing, thoughtful, and spiritual woman. That's what I wanted. In my mind, I thought it would happen another way. However, that wasn't meant for me, that wasn't God's plan for me. I wanted to help others, write to inspire, and start my own business. Looking at my circumstances, it didn't look like that would ever happen, so I started small. I always loved to journal as a child as it was cathartic for me, so I started there. Later, I began my own blog. Many times, we feel if we don't have a large audience, it doesn't mean much to anyone but I firmly believe that whoever is meant to cross your path, will.

Self-Love

Self-love is something I never heard of until I was in my thirties. I was one of those that felt if you give, give, give, eventually someone would love you back. I had to learn to take care of me. When you don't love yourself, you will be very open to others to define you and come into your life and do damage. Now, when I say self-love I don't mean arrogance. I define self-love as knowing who you are, loving yourself enough to have boundaries, and using your gifts and talents to light the world. When you allow yourself to be abused is the opposite of self-love. I realize when I loved myself more I would attract more love and that I would also know when to walk away from what was not love.

Rewriting My Story

The story we tell ourselves daily is the life we will lead. For many years of my life, my story was this: I was abused and abandoned because I wasn't good enough, smart enough, or pretty enough. I was depressed. I made poor choices and thought that a good man would never want or love me. Just thinking of that story makes me cringe. "Perception is the only reality." "What you focus on expands." Now, I see that those lies are what I allowed myself to believe and so that reality was attracted to me and I accepted it. It was time to change my story. My new story is: I am a determined, smart, lovable, and a successful mother of three beautiful children. I am a woman that has overcome, learned, and inspire others by facing my challenges head on. I have more good that is available to me than I can imagine. God loves me and I love me. I open my heart to love more and more each day and I have found that it is important to be open and willing for change to happen in life.

One technique I learned is to look in a mirror each morning and tell myself how much I love myself. I know it sounds simple enough but for someone who never understood self-love and who always tried to seek love externally, it was very hard in the beginning. The first time I began to tell myself how much I loved and adored ME, I looked in the mirror and cried. It was such an odd and unusual feeling because it was very new. For me to make the transition, it was something I had to do every day for a while, until it became a little easier. Eventually, I discovered that I was feeling a lot better about myself. I would encourage anyone struggling with life limitations and self-worth, to try the "I love me," experience.

Breathe In, Breathe Out

Overcoming depression, loneliness, and other emotional limitations is something I will always be working on throughout my life. There are times when those old negative emotions will rise in me. The key is learning my triggers, continue my self-love practices, and focus on my gifts. I had to learn that every day is a new opportunity unfolding for me. I give myself a break, understanding that I am always learning and growing and will never be perfect. I will never compare myself or my life to anyone else's. Mark Twain said, "Comparison is the death of joy."

I choose to live in peace. I know now that it is not my job to react to everyday things that people do that hurt me. I don't seek revenge or get angry when people choose to walk out of my life. I simply strive to be the best person that I can be and let God do the rest. That is what I live by. I'm not saying there aren't days when I don't become angry, scared, or have sad moments but the difference is that I understand how to deal with those emotions. There are times when it is good to just sit down and breathe. It is so important to find what works for you. It could be exercising, walking, journaling, talking, meditating, or even listening to music…just find what works for you.

One of my favorite references to shift my emotions is, "Where is the next wonderful thing?" This allows my mind to start seeking the answers for whatever challenge I may be facing. It doesn't mean it will be fixed in one day but regardless of how long it takes for the shift to happen, I refuse to allow myself to go into that place of depression and hopelessness. I simply wait for the next wonderful thing.

I learned to let go of the guilt I felt by distancing myself from my family. Ultimately, I don't expect any more than they can give me and my happiness is up to me and no one else. I get to choose the love I want in my life and walking away from drama is just a demonstration of that choice. On this journey of life, everyone comes to that point when they say enough is enough. I must live my dream for me. There are always people around that will try to convince you otherwise. The amazing thing is that you don't have to listen to them. We have a wonderful part of our body called the mind, and you can decide to believe what you want about you.

Many times, fear can paralyze people, keeping them from ever following their dreams. Then, out of their own pain, they try to place that same fear on others because, as they say, misery loves company. We must realize that there will be naysayers, but your journey must go on. I realize that my dreams are mine alone and a gift given to me by God to share with the world. I also had to learn who I was and how to love myself. It turns out that those dreams of being a singer or dancer were someone else's dreams that I had borrowed for a time until I learned to fall in love with me, my life, and my journey. I had to ask God to connect me to other big dreamers, so that I could have the support I needed to make my dreams come true. Therefore, when I realized it was all possible, I recognized that I was heading down the right path because I had seen what that looks like in the people I surround myself with. It has been a spiritual shift in my life. I realize where true joy comes from, from the inside out. We all face obstacles, come across broken people but knowing who you are is the key. Believing in the dream God has for your life, focusing on the vision for your life gives you a strength to face your fears, overcome obstacles, and tap into your God-given inner strength.

Spiritual Crisis

Demetria Hill Cannady, PhD, LPC

Spiritual crisis is when an individual has a significant and drastic life change which alters their spiritual beliefs, attitudes, focus, passion or purpose. This change may cause a major disruption in the individual's emotional state, psychological, physiological, and social state of mind. Some spiritual crisis can cause psychiatric complications such as:

- Mystical experiences
- New religious movements and cults
- Psychic opening
- Visionary experience
- Kundalini awakening
- Near-death experience
- Possession experience
- Shamanic crisis
- Loss of faith
- Alien encounters/ Paranormal experience
- Terminal and Life-threatening illness
- Changes in membership, practices, and beliefs.

Depression

Demetria Hill Cannady, PhD, LPC

Depression is an issue which has plagued every person at least once in their lives. There is a difference in depression and clinical depression. There is situational depression which consists of a situation, person, or event causing one to become sad, have anxieties, or become depressed. In situational depression, you will have these feeling briefly lasting no more than a few weeks. Situational depression will occur from life events such as temporary financial strain, ending a relationship, divorce, retirement, loss of a job, death of a family member or friend. However, when your situational depression begins to exceed more than two weeks, then you may be headed to a more significant form of Depression titled Clinical Depression.

Most African Americans will say that they are experiencing "the blues" when they become depressed, but as stated earlier, if the depression exceeds more than two weeks, then it is no longer just "the blues". At this stage, Clinical Depression begins to affect your thought process, actions, moods, and behaviors. Some individuals become withdrawn and irritable while others may be mad at the world. Research reports that there are more than nineteen million Americans who suffer from depression, in some form. Depression is a thief which robs individuals of the happiness which one should experience daily.

There are symptoms of clinical depression:

- Cognitive issues (irrational and/or negative thoughts)
- Genetic factors (predisposition)
- Gender (more women suffer from depression than men
- Medications
- Physical Illnesses (inability to do activities which the individual was previously able to do).

- Medications (side-effects)
- Life situations (death; loss of parent, significant other/spouse, empty nest)

There are symptoms of clinical depression and if you or someone you know has experienced at least five or more of these symptoms for more than two weeks, it may be wise to contact your primary care professional or a therapist:

- A persistent sad, anxious, or "empty" mood, or excessive crying
- Reduced appetite and weight loss or increased appetite and weight gain
- Persistent physical symptoms that do not respond to treatment, such as headaches, digestive disorders, and chronic pain
- Irritability, restlessness
- Decreased energy, fatigue, feeling "slowed down"
- Feelings of guilt, worthlessness, helplessness, hopelessness, and pessimism
- Sleeping too much or too little, early morning waking
- Loss of interest or pleasure activities, including sex
- Difficulty concentrating, remembering, or making decisions
- Thoughts of death or suicide or suicide attempts

*Symptoms are Courtesy of American Psychiatric Association

With psychotherapy and/or psychotropic medication, your depressive symptoms should disappear. Psychotherapy helps to address the root of the depression and assist you with developing coping techniques to combat the depression. Psychotropic medications, specifically antidepressants, which triggers the chemicals in the brain and improves the depressed moods. Some antidepressants take up to eight weeks prior to you seeing a difference so it is best to take the medication as prescribed for optimal results. Antidepressants are NOT habit forming.

American Psychiatric Association (2013). Diagnostic and statistical manual of mental disorders, 5th Ed. Washington, DC.

 Tanyala L. Calloway has been married to Bennie E. Calloway III, for 22 years. They have two daughters, Hannah Alexis and Kayla Savannah. Tanyala graduated from Valdosta High School in 1988 and attended college in New Jersey and Valdosta State University obtaining a Counseling Degree. She has worked in the field on Long-Term HealthCare for 23 years and presently works for Pruitt Healthcare in Valdosta, Georgia as the Activities Director and Volunteer Coordinator. Tanyala was voted as Activity Director of the Year in 2004 for the Georgia Healthcare Association. She also served as State President for two years for GSNNHAD and has received several awards.

Tanyala is a member of the National Council for Negro Women and serves as Chaplain. She is also a member of the Hahira-Lowndes County Cotillion (Debutantes) Committee. Tanyala is an active supporter of the March of Dimes and Lupus Association. She participates in Relay for Life, Alzheimer's Association, Camp Cocoon, and United Hospice. Tanyala is a member of Trinity Missionary Baptist Church in Boston, Georgia where her husband is the Pastor and she serves on the Praise and Worship Team. She is also the Director for the Dance Team and serves on the Intercessory Prayer Team. Tanyala loves people, loves to shop, read, pray, travel, help and serve others. She is a proud member of Theta Phi Sigma Christian Sorority, Inc., where she serves as Chaplain for her local chapter. Her favorite scripture is, "For I shall not die, but live, and declare the works of the Lord." Tanyala is an overcomer and "Victorious" is her name.

"For I Shall Not Die, but LIVE!"

TANYALA CALLOWAY

In the year 2000, I attended aerobics classes three times a week. I seemed to always feel more tired than usual, and I thought it was just because I was out of shape. Not only during the aerobics classes, but I felt a lot more tired throughout the day. One day, after a month of attending the classes, while I was at work at Shady Acres Nursing Home in Douglas, Ga., I felt more tired, and fatigue was taking over me. It took me so long to get up out of a chair; it was a struggle to stand up. I literally felt like an "Old Elderly Woman." The fatigue and the tiredness seemed to get worse so I decided to inform my boss of how I was feeling. She started asking me questions out of concern and when I told her my symptoms, she looked at me and stated, "That sounds like some kind of arthritis condition, but you need to go to the doctor." I agreed with her. I made the appointment and my doctor at that time tested me for everything. All the tests came back normal or negative. He finally said, "Mrs. Calloway, there is only one thing left to test you for, and that is Lupus." When the test came back, the doctor confirmed my diagnosis to me and that is when my whole life changed. My life was changed by one diagnosis, Lupus! Tears began to fall from my eyes because I thought that I was going to die. I had no idea what LUPUS was or how I got it. I had so many questions. I returned to my job the next day and informed my boss of my diagnosis. She hugged me so tight, and she also informed me that everything would be alright. My boss also informed me that having Lupus did not mean I was going to die. She knew others who were diagnosed with Lupus, and they were living great lives. Well, to be very honest, I did not want to hear those words at that time. I just wanted the Lupus to go away! Of course, I knew in my spirit that I needed to press my way and move forward!

I continued to go to work every day knowing that I had been diagnosed with this crucial disease, but I had to do my job to the best of my ability. I worked as an Activity Director, which consisted of me planning and coordinating activities for the residents to help maintain their Quality of Life. I loved making them smile even when I didn't feel like smiling myself. I had a smile on my face, but physically I felt weak and tired. I hid my feelings well! There were a few of my coworkers who could see that something was not quite right. I continued to press my way and after a few months, I had a flare-up which caused the doctor to admit me in the hospital. This flare-up affected my muscles and joints. The disease attacked my body so bad that I could not wipe my own face. It was a struggle but I made it through. I was living in Douglas, Georgia during all of this, and all my immediate family were living in Valdosta, Georgia.

One of my closest friends who was also a member of my church came to visit with me in the hospital every day even though I lived in Douglas at the time. I was unable to walk at times due to my legs being very weak, and because my arms also were very weak, my husband had to feed me every meal. I remember being in such pain, especially when I got up to walk to the bathroom. I kept going and I didn't give up. Every day was a struggle for me, I was praying, crying, and asking God, "Why me?" At one point, I thought I was going to die! I wanted to be home! After a few weeks of being in the hospital, the doctors allowed me to go home to recover. I had not been in the hospital since I was small child, so this was an experience I will never forget.

In 2003, I began to have baby feelings; Yes, I wanted to have a baby. I talked it over with my doctor, and I did not get the response I wanted to hear. My doctor felt that it would be a bad idea for me to have a baby because of my diagnosis. He informed me that the pregnancy would be high- risk, and I probably would have a lot of problems with the pregnancy. I had that feeling again and felt like I was going to die just hearing him say to me that I shouldn't have a baby. I heard him, but I refused to let his words get in my spirit. My husband and I tried to get pregnant, and then we waited! We tried and we waited! After nine months of trying, I still was not pregnant. We went to the doctor again, and he told us to try one more thing before we take the next step to help me get pregnant. The doctor told us that he believed that I was trying too hard, and I needed to relax my mind.

We decided to take a trip to New Orleans to "relax," it was where we had desired to go for a long time. We drove all the way to New Orleans from Valdosta, Georgia, but halfway there, we had to pull over to the side of the highway because of the hail storm. This was my first experience with hail. It was falling and hitting our car like rocks! I thought the hail was going to break our windshield, so I started to pray that we would get through this storm. I also prayed and asked God to bless my womb and allow me to give birth to a child that we could have as our own. I just could not believe that God would allow me to marry this man and not be able to give him children. I just could not believe it! Once the hail storm stopped, we continued to drive to our destination. During our stay in New Orleans; we shopped, ate good food, walked the famous Bourbon Street, and enjoyed the many special events and activities. We enjoyed each other and rested our minds. I could hear God speak to my spirit and say, "LIVE, LOVE, AND LAUGH!" We decided not to talk about our jobs, church, or anything that would cause stress. A lot of people do not realize that stress is a silent killer. You can be stressed and not realize it. There are many things that can cause stress, so since we were not quite sure what was causing our stress, we just decided to talk about good and positive things. We just enjoyed being with each other! I love Dr. Bennie E. Calloway III, so just being with him with some extra fun and laughs made it even better. We had a blast!

When we returned home to Georgia, it was at my next doctor's appointment that my husband and I would get the great news, "Mrs. Calloway, You're pregnant!" I was so happy and excited, and I gave God a big praise! I began to thank God for the miracle! I cried tears of joy because I knew God did it. And yes, the baby was conceived in New Orleans! Sometimes to get something you've never had, you must do something you've never done! New Orleans will always be a special place for me and my husband. It was my faith in God that allowed me not to give up on something that I desired. I believe God's Word that says, "Delight yourself in the Lord, and He will give you the desires of your heart," so I believe that God heard my cry, and because I didn't allow the enemy to cause me to doubt, I came out victorious!

As I carried this unborn child, I felt so blessed. I was high-risk, so I had several doctors' appointments. The pregnancy seemed to go well during my first six months. During my seventh month, I went to one of my appointments, the doctor was concerned about my baby's weight and there were some other major concerns. He said, "Mrs. Calloway, the baby has not gained any weight since your last visit." He said that he saw some other things that were major concerns to him. I remember, he said to me these words, "Mrs. Calloway, I am going to send you to Savannah to be admitted to the hospital there to monitor you and have more tests done." My husband drove us there, and I was admitted. The next day, later that evening, my husband had to drive back to

Valdosta, Georgia because he had to handle some important business for us. Not long after my husband left, the nurse came in my room and stated, "We have to take the baby right now. The doctor said for us to take you back to get you ready." The doctor came in my room, I called my husband and told him to turn around because they were about to give me a C-Section to take the baby. He got nervous, but he turned around right away. The doctors decided to wait for my husband to get back to the hospital. It seemed like forever! I began having an anxiety attack, and I could not breathe properly. They put me on oxygen, and I was still struggling to breathe. My husband finally arrived and quickly they took me to the back for the surgery.

The birth was a beautiful experience! Being able to just lay there while the doctor cuts your stomach, reach in, and pull out a beautiful creation. A beautiful baby girl, Hannah Alexis Calloway was born on May 2, 2004, weighing 1 lb. 11 oz. To God be the Glory for this awesome miracle baby, and she belongs to me. Most premature babies must have oxygen to help them breathe, but our Hannah did not need oxygen at all. Wow! We were so amazed at this. Our little Hannah was ready to fight to live! This was one of the toughest times of my life. Our little princess had to stay in the hospital for five and half weeks. I stayed at the Ronald McDonald House which was directly across from the hospital. The Ronald McDonald House allows mothers who give birth to premature babies to live there while their babies heal, grow, and get better to go home.

My husband and I did not know what to expect. The first day, I witnessed a mother holding her premature baby in her arms. The mother was rocking the baby while walking back and forth in one of the hallways. The mother's baby passed away, and she had a tough time accepting it. It was like the mother was praying for her baby to wake up. After witnessing this, I got nervous! I asked myself, "Is my baby going to die?" I would cry, cry, and cry! My husband would go to the hospital chapel to pray several times a day for the first week. I decided to breast feed but Hannah's mouth was so small, she had trouble latching on to my nipple. I had to walk to the hospital across the street to sit in the Pump Room to pump milk from my breasts. The hospital stored the milk so I could feed her on schedule. The breast milk was the best milk for her to have at that time. Hannah began to grow and could graduate to the next unit. Our prayers were being answered. She was growing! Glory to God! The time was finally here…. time for Hannah to go home. Hannah experienced one apnea attack in which she stopped breathing for a second or two, so they ordered a heart monitor to go home with her. The doctors said that she would have to use the heart monitor until she was six months old. When we took Hannah to her next check-up, the doctors examined her and stated, "This baby does not need this machine." The doctor informed us that her heart was good and strong! Again, God gets another praise!

We had to travel back and forth to Nahunta, Georgia to see how she was developing, such as her brain. After a few times of traveling there, the doctors told us that we did not have to bring her back because there was nothing wrong with her. She was developing well. Hannah responded well, her memory was good, she was alert when she was supposed to be, her bones were developed and strong, and she passed all the little tests. The doctors thought that Hannah might be delayed in some things because of her prematurity. An example, her taking longer to walk. Well, hear this, they thought she might not walk until she was closer to two years old, but Hannah started walking at ten months old. Our Hannah is an overcomer! We are so very proud of our Hannah. She is now thirteen years old and loves to eat! When Hannah was nine months old, I found out that I was pregnant again. I was pregnant with another girl, Kayla Savannah, who was born 4 lbs. on October 8, 2005.

Well, when I found out that I was pregnant again, I was devastated! I did not think that I could do it. Hannah was nine months old, and I was pregnant again. I cried a lot and suffered from Post-Partum Depression. I thought about aborting the baby, but my husband simply told me these words, "If you kill my baby, I will leave you!" Well, that's all it took for me to keep this baby. I was going to learn to accept it and do my best to raise my children to the best of my ability. My mother, Clara Daniels, told me, "If God did not think that you could do it, He would not have allowed it to happen. You will be a great mother of two." The day came when I gave birth to my beautiful Kayla! Kayla was a cry baby, and I had to rock her to sleep a lot. She kept me and daddy up a lot of nights. There was one night which I remember, Kayla was crying and did not want to go to sleep. I was very tired and sleepy! I remember clearly while I was sitting in the baby's room, I was holding Kayla in my arm and I looked at her and started praying for her. I felt a peace come upon me and realized that Kayla has a purpose for being here.

After a few years of being a mother, which I enjoy so very much, it was 2011, and I was feeling bad. I had a very bad cold which lasted too long for a normal cold. I went to the doctor, and he said it was a common cold. He sent me home on regular cold medicines, etc. Well, the medicine did not seem to work. And I was getting worse! One Saturday morning, I felt worse than I ever did in my life. I just didn't feel right at all, so I told my husband and he asked, "Do you need to go the hospital?" I replied, "Yes, I think I do." I called my sister to come and pick me up while my husband stayed at home with the girls. When I got to the hospital, after being seen the doctor gives me the verdict, "You have pneumonia!" I was so amazed to hear this, but I felt like it was true. The doctor admitted me into the hospital. My bloodwork was so abnormal! I could not do anything for myself. My husband, Dr. Bennie Calloway, III, my mother, Clara Daniels, and my best friend, Fredina Berrian, came to the hospital to help feed me. The Nurses and Aides bathed and dressed me because the pneumonia caused me to have another flare-up. It was during this flare-up that life as I knew it seemed to be over for me. The doctors stated to me, "Mrs. Calloway, your body does seem to be responding the medication that you're taking. We are giving the highest dosage of steroids that we can give you. We can only think of one other thing that may help."

Both my regular family doctor and my specialist had given up hope on me but I did not give up on myself. I cried and prayed all day long. I was hospitalized for six weeks. The "enemy" wanted me to give up. I read God's Word and spoke it in my spirit. One scripture in the Bible became my all-time favorite, "For I shall not Die, but LIVE, and declare the works of the Lord." I spoke this scripture several times a day. The hospital finally released me from the hospital with little hope of returning to work or walking! The doctor said that I will probably have to participate in physical therapy at home to walk again. I was devastated at first and then I had to remember my scripture, "For I shall not Die, but LIVE!" When I got home, I saw a wheelchair that someone brought to my house. I told my husband not bring it in the house because I would not be needing it. I will walk again!

I was a little depressed which was showing in my attitude and actions. My muscles were so weak, and my husband had to help me do everything. It just seemed like I was giving up. My husband bought me this gospel CD which had a song called "Encourage Yourself." My husband said to me, "This is for you! Now listen to it in here by yourself." He walked out and left me alone. I listened to it several times, and it literally lifted my spirit so high. I cried and praised God like never before. I felt the Spirit of God upon me like a warm towel. God's presence surrounded me, and I felt stronger! I prayed to God these words, "God, I will do what I can do and you do what I can't do!" I continued, "I am healed in Jesus Name! And I shall not Die, but LIVE!" The doctor ordered for me to have a private physical therapist which would come to my house and help me get my muscles strong. The therapist came and did her job. I was determined and ready to get better. I did exactly what the therapist told me to do, while praying and asking God to give me the strength to do what she required me to do. My therapist was impressed with my determination and great attitude!

After a few weeks, I was giving myself a bath, walking in the kitchen, cooking my own food, getting up out of the bed on my own, and just walking down my hallway with no assistance. To me, it seemed like a miracle! I was at home and received physical therapy for two months. After the therapist released me, I returned to work one month later. When I was sitting on my couch one day, I told the Lord, "If you heal and bring me out of this, I will shout out and give you all of the Glory for it!" I promised God that I would let others know that He healed me! I quoted my favorite scripture every day out loud. I believe if you speak it out loud, it will manifest quicker!! I believed the saying that you have "Say It til' You See It!"

I had two visions that I kept close in my spirit. First, I was going to return to work and walk in through the front doors with no wheelchair and no assistance. Second, I was going to dance and shout in church again like never before. They both came to pass! Glory to God! I will never forget my first day back to work. My husband put me out in front of the building. One of my coworkers, Alicia Nocent, was standing there waiting and looking at me. The only thing she did was open the door for me. I walked in the building with a praise! Alicia was smiling so big, and she was very happy to see me come back to work. I was happy to get back to work because I love my job.

It seemed like a new beginning! I was back at work and my coworkers lovingly welcomed me back, along with my residents who were overflowing with joy! I was so ready to work, but the doctor told me to take it slow. I was still moving slow, but I was grateful to God that I could move and walk! I did have to roll up the halls in a wheelchair. As weeks went by, I was very happy to be at work, but the enemy tried to attack my mind about my weight loss. There were several people who made statements about my weight loss. There were some cruel statements which were said that would make anyone feel down and depressed. I allowed those statements to cause me to go into a spirit of low self-esteem. I suffered with this "bad" spirit for a long time.

When I looked in the mirror, I did not think that I was pretty or beautiful because of my weight loss. To me, I looked skinny and ugly! I really had it bad! My depression got so bad until it started to affect my marriage. I would go hide from my husband when I had to change clothes so that he could not see my body. I didn't want to have sex with him because I thought my body was too skinny for him to look at. I thought he would change his mind about making love to me if he saw my skinny body. I finally felt led to talk to my mother and one of my best friends at work. I shared with them what I was struggling with, and they both agreed that it was just an attack of the enemy. They both told me that my husband loved me and they believed that he did not have a problem with my body. It was just all in my own mind. I remember my mother telling me to go shopping and buy something sexy to wear to bed. She told me to buy something that I felt sexy in because if I felt sexy, then he would think I was sexy. My mother stated to me, "Baby, he's a man! A man just wants his needs to be met, and you have the tools to meet his needs, so use them!"

It took me a few weeks to follow her instructions but I finally did. I began to pray and ask God to help me. I did not want "this" to destroy my marriage. One day, my husband came to me for no reason and said these words to me, "Baby, you are so beautiful!" My eyes stretched and my heart melted! I grabbed him and kissed him! However, I still isolated myself from him. I continued to pray. One day my best friend, Fredina Berrian, called me. She knew something was going on because she felt it in her spirit. After I told her what I was struggling with, she gave it to me good. Fredina told me to go shop for something sexy, and she offered to take me shopping to make sure I brought something sexy. She was part of my emotional support system. Fredina encouraged me daily. She prayed for me over the phone and spoke words of empowerment into my spirit. I started to feel a lifting in my spirit. I felt better and better as the days went by. I finally followed my mother and Fredina's instructions. I decided to surprise my husband one night and the rest is history! Yes, it was a magical night and has been ever since that night. Our marriage is stronger than it has ever been. Our love for each other is deeper because of the struggle. I love my handsome man, Dr. Bennie E. Calloway III. I give God the glory for how He has strengthened our union together. We do not let a day go by without a kiss, hug, and words of love. We keep the fire burning!

It seemed as if the blessings just continued to flow. The Lord not only blessed our marriage but God blessed my husband's ministry. After much criticism, "put downs," back-biting, judging spirits, two-faced friends, and being left for dead, my husband's ministry has blossomed like never before. He was blessed with a new church, Trinity Missionary Baptist Church in Boston, Georgia and recently released his new book, "Deeper Awareness,' which is doing very well. We are so excited about what God is doing in our lives. We thanked God for sending people in our lives who truly love and support us. God sent people in our lives who believe in us and love us for who we are. God has shown us loving kindness, grace, and mercy that we did not deserve! God has moved mightily in our lives.

God has performed a miracle in my body like never before! During the month of March 2017, I had a doctor appointment for a regular check-up. I am usually calm when I go to the doctor, but this visit was different. I was unusually happy and excited. I felt a peace like I never had before. The doctor's visit went well. After the completion of my lab work, I went home with an assurance in knowing that my bloodwork was going to be good. Another week went by and I was scheduled to have an infusion done for my bones. While I was waiting in the room for the nurse to come, I began to pray and praise God! I prayed for God to bless the infusion and that I would not have any side effects from it. I prayed that infusion would do what it was made to do and nothing less. I quoted my favorite scripture again, "For I shall not die, but LIVE, and declare the works of God!

The nurse finally came in and stood directly in front of me. She said that she wanted to go over a few things before she started the infusion. She was smiling so that was a good sign. She stated these words to me, "Mrs. Calloway, before we can do this infusion, your labs have to be good and normal. Well, yours are very good. All your labs are great! According to this, you are nowhere near flaring-up! We can start your infusion, if you are ready?" I started tearing up because that was sweet news to my ears. I do not hear news like that from my doctor very often so God deserved that Praise! As soon as I left the doctor, I called my husband and my mom. They both were very excited to hear the great news. My mom said, "God just keeps on blessing you baby, go ahead and praise Him because He deserves it!" I called a few other family and friends to share my good news as well. I remember it was during this time that I began to receive an abundance of phone calls from different churches and individuals. They wanted me to come and share my testimony or be the Mistress of Ceremony which always gave me a chance to give my testimony. God was opening so many doors for me to share and declare His Works! God is so Worthy of the Praise and He deserves the Praise! He deserves my Best Praise, Hallelujah God!

God has truly been good to me! He has been there for me during my journey. My story continues because I will continue to bless others with my testimony. I will continue to pray for others who are sick and afflicted with disease. I will never forget that I promised God in 2011 that if He healed me, I would declare to others what He has done for me. I will declare that God is a healer! Others need to know that God is a healer! Others need to know that they must believe and not doubt! Respect the doctor's diagnosis but don't claim it! My words of wisdom to others and for myself- this is what I say and tell others, "I was given a diagnosis, but I don't have anything! I am not sick, but healed, in Jesus Name! I claim my healing daily! Healing is my Name! Victory is my Name! I am a winner! I am a conqueror! I am a fighter! I am a soldier in the Army of the Lord! I am a Warrior! I am a Victor, and not a Victim! "I shall not die, but LIVE!"

Postpartum Depression

Demetria Hill Cannady, PhD, LPC

Postpartum depression is a form of depression which affects women after childbirth. The mothers normally have depression which extends beyond having "the blues" as most folks call it. The "blues" may be brief worry, unhappiness, or fatigue following the birth of a child and typically last no more than one to two weeks. Postpartum depression can affect women by causing extreme sadness, anxieties, and exhaustion from being the caretaker of a new born baby. This depression affects daily activities in the aspects of experiencing difficulties with should be "normal" day-to-day tasks (bathing, eating, cooking, caring for their family, etc.).

Postpartum depression is caused by a combination of physical and emotional factors. After childbirth, the levels of hormones (estrogen and progesterone) in a woman's body quickly drop. This causes chemical changes in the brain that may trigger mood swings. In addition, many mothers are unable to get the rest they need to fully recover from giving birth. Constant sleep deprivation can lead to physical discomfort and exhaustion, which can contribute to the symptoms of postpartum depression (www.nimh.nih.gov).

Symptoms of Postpartum Depression

- Feeling sad, empty, hopeless, or overwhelmed
- Crying more often than usual and/or for no apparent reason
- Excessive worry or over anxiousness
- Irritable, moody, and/or restlessness
- Sleeping too much and too often
- Unable to concentrate, difficulty remembering, and indecisive decision-making skills
- Intense anger and/or rage
- Loss of interest in activities and/or people
- Frequent bodily pains

- Overeating/ undereating
- Isolating self from family and friends
- Unattached or poor attachment to the baby
- Thoughts of suicide/homicide following birth of the baby (www.nimh.nih.gov)

Women Who Are More Prone to Postpartum Depression

- Depression during pregnancy or postpartum following previous pregnancies
- Diagnosis of Depression and/or Bipolar Disorder prior to pregnancy
- Family history of depression or other mental illness
- A stressful life event which may have occurred during the pregnancy or shortly after delivery
- Medical complications (with child or self) during or after childbirth
- Unhappy feelings as it related to the pregnancy
- Little to no emotional support from friends and family
- Alcohol/ drug issues, past and/or present (www.nimh.nih.gov)

***If you or someone you know may be experiencing symptoms of Postpartum Depression, please speak with your primary physician to discuss treatment options.**

 Gena Golden is a Licensed Clinical Social Worker, psychotherapist, speaker, trainer, coach, hypnotherapist, and author. She is a mother of two bright and creative teenagers and has been married over 20 years to her best friend, Dr. Jones, a college professor. Mrs. Golden received her Bachelors of Social Work (BSW) from Temple University in 1991 and her Masters of Social Work (MSW) from Clark Atlanta University Whitney B. Young, Jr. School of Social Work in 1993. She received her certification in hypnotherapy in 2014.

As a practicing psychotherapist at *Inner Coach Counseling, LLC*, in her private practice located in Atlanta, Georgia, Mrs. Golden works primarily with women to help decrease the symptoms of depression, anxiety, self-esteem and self-sabotaging behaviors to name a few. Mrs. Golden embraces a holistic (mind, body and spirit) therapeutic approach to help her clients discover their inner wisdom to transform their lives. In practice, Mrs. Golden uses an eclectic approach to care such as Cognitive Behavioral Therapy, Mindfulness, Hypnotherapy and Solution Focused Therapy.

Prior to opening her private practice, Mrs. Golden was the Founder and Director of an agency for adults with intellectual disabilities for several years providing community access services, residential services, supportive employment and life sharing programs. Additionally, she has amassed over 23 years of combined experience providing individual and group therapy, crisis intervention, developmental/intellectual disabilities, bereavement and grief counseling, services to the homeless and transient population, substance abuse treatment, DUI clinical evaluations, forensic social work, social security disability evaluations and chronic and severe mental health disorders.

Her most recent endeavor includes working with mental health professionals overcome test anxiety. She has a private Facebook group and an e-course entitled

'A *Holistic Approach to Overcoming Test Anxiety'* will be launched soon.

Mrs. Golden also creates customized guided imagery MP3 and CD's for pregnant women, athletes and others with specific problems and blockages.

She is currently co-authoring a book entitled, 'Authentic Tales', a compilation of stories from spiritual leaders and helping professionals. Additionally, she has received training as a Doula, Reiki Practitioner, Certified Crystal Reader and Energy Medicine.

Her training and speaking topics include:

- Intellectual Disabilities
- Cultural Considerations on End of Life Care
- Test Taking Anxiety
- The Power of the Subconscious Mind
- Eliminating the Inner Critic and Embracing and Inner Coach for Success
- Adoption Home Studies

Lastly, Mrs. Golden is a member of the National Association of Social Workers (NASW), Association of Black Social Workers (ABSW), American Association of Black Psychologists (ABPsi), Atlanta Metro Black Chamber of Commerce (AMBCC), Georgia Therapy Network (GTN), Metro Atlanta Therapist Network (MATN) and the International Federation of Hypnotherapist.

For more information:

Gena Golden, CHT, LCSW

Coach, speaker, trainer, psychotherapist and hypnotherapist. She helps clients overcome self-sabotage, depression and anxiety (including Test Anxiety)

Inner Coach Counseling, LLC
Atlanta, Georgia

Www.InnerCoachHypnotherapy.com
Www.facebook.com/InnerCoachATL
Info@Innercoachhypnothrepay.com
877-430-3828

Slay Your Inner Critic

Gena Golden, CHT, LCSW

When I was very young, living in Philadelphia, I did not understand the power that words and thoughts had on my life. I joined in on the harmful familial and community vernacular of my environment; not understanding the implications that later impacted my development as an adult. Criticism of others and self-deprecating language were commonplace. Philadelphians often referred to their own city as 'Filthy-delphia' because of the tons of trash strewn on the sidewalks and streets. Saying that it was filthy, then thinking and believing the same, led to the unconscious behavior of throwing more trash on the ground. As a child, we called our infamous Schuylkill River, "Schuylkill Punch", which implied (rightfully so) that the water was dirty and bad to drink. The racial tension, segregation, dirty environment, criminal violence, and potholes confirmed feelings of low self-worth.

Consequently, being raised in the inner city, most children exude a level of 'toughness' in order to manage the 'mean streets' of Philly. We knew early on that as long as you were on your own block surrounded by your friends and neighbors, you were safe. We knew that our friends 'had our back.' Unfortunately, one day when I was about 12 years old, my friends and I were about the serious business of jumping rope in the middle of the street one summer day. A car load of white boys in a convertible, sped down our street disturbing our Double Dutch game. One of the white boys leaned out of the car and spat right in the center of my friend Stephanie's' forehead! As the spittle ran down her face, she stood there in shock. We were all mortified. As Stephanie cried, I knew then that it was not safe for me to be totally carefree. The impact of that experience seemed to put everyone on high alert after that and as a little girl, this violation of our humanity made me question my safety and worthiness. Hence, I decided that viewing the world through 'rosey' glasses was not a viable option if I wanted to live, thrive and survive in Philly.

Despite its faults, Philly was not all bad. It did have an upside. Traditionally, it was affectionately called, 'The City of Brotherly Love' and it was known for its scrumptious Italian bread, hoagies, warm salted pretzels, beautiful architecture and fine dining restaurants. Even though my childhood environment was filled with some very, scary events, I experienced tons of fun, laughter and great memories with my parents, sisters, brother and a close network of neighborhood friends (with whom I still adore!).

An illustration of my childhood experiences demonstrate how pessimistic and cynical thought patterns are developed which negatively impact a worldview. It exemplifies how early experiences can condition the mind, and it holds us back from bringing forth our divine gifts. As a result of my childhood experiences, my young mind was conditioned to think and embrace limiting beliefs that could have permanently prevented me from achieving any level of success. It is apparent that unhealthy thoughts are the likely culprit to mental bondage and fear.

Hence, it is my hope that my contribution to this book will in some small way, inspire you to change the way you think, speak and behave for a better life. Norman Vincent Peale is quoted as saying, "Change your thoughts and you change your world." I agree with the wisdom of this statement. What I am sharing with you is my personal *her*story. My herstory or journey may be similar to yours. It is a journey of self-discovery, growth and transformation of my mind. A journey of personal evolution and change.

It begins, in part, with self-limiting thinking and negative self-talk and evolved into a process of *remembering* my capacity to change. My story is not about blaming or making someone responsible for my life. It is a story about how I learned to accept my frailties and the frailties of others through non-judgmental self-compassion. In the process, I learned to transcend the old patterns of negative subconscious programming that no longer support me. My quest is to understand the utility of my past experiences, yet knowing that I can choose to be released from the oppressive thoughts about thoughts experiences.

Subsequently, my self-work includes speaking consciously, deliberately and choosing my thoughts wisely. While this is the case, my journey has not been perfect. There has been slip ups and setbacks. I have had errors in my thinking and behaviors. Healing, I've come to understand, is an ongoing process, a lifelong journey. And like you, I am a work in progress who is ever growing and transforming. My hope is that my story will spark a flame in you to ignite the courage to shift your mindset and free you from the inner critic that could be holding you back.

The Birth of the Inner Critic

I was raised in a fun-loving, close knit but very critical family. My loving parents loved to dance and play sports. My mother was a giver. She was athletic, artistic and fun-loving. She was a natural born teacher and entrepreneur. Everyone loved her. My dad, a former amateur Negro Baseball League player and hard worker loved sports and had an awesome sense of humor (when he was mad about something). Unfortunately, my mother made her transition when I was a student at Temple University in 1987 and my dad died just 3 months after my first-born child arrived in 1999. My sisters and brother and I remain close knit. I talk to my oldest sister almost daily. Even as children, we were like four peas in a pod.

Subsequently, the criticisms my siblings and I doled out on one another were cloaked with humor and sarcasm. We laughed at the verbal jabs while cleverly setting up our next 'funny' attack like rapid fire aimed at the offender. We called this "busting" on one another. Imagine the banter between J.J and Thelma on the show *Good Times*. That was us! Back and forth the humorous and sometime wounding attacks went on at the expense of the other. "Your eyes are so big!" or "Your hair is so nappy!" or "You are so *BLACK*!" Jokes had no boundaries. Everything about us was vulnerable to attack; no holds barred. This was how it was back then. Not only did this behavior occur in my family but in my neighbor, at school and in the community.

Why did we throw harsh criticisms at one another? Was it self-loathing or internalized oppression. Looking back, I am able to clearly see the etiology of why people condemn themselves and others. When I look at my own life, my negative self-talk probably started soon after my birth.

Furthermore, my grandmother, rest her soul, would tell stories about my birth. I was born on the early morning of Halloween. My birth apparently disrupted the normal "trick or treat" activities planned annually by my family. My birth would change the dynamic of the family. It would either balance the scales or cause one side to be weighted down on the "too many girls" side of the scale. Having me would determine if our family would have two boys and two girls or three girls and one boy. Needless to say, I was a girl! The youngest of four. The scales were unbalanced. When I arrived, my grandmother would later tell me that she said, "Well, we got the *witch*, now all we need is a broom!" She cracked up at the thought. I never thought this was funny. I was always disturbed by this story but did not know why. My brother accused me of being too sensitive or not having a sense of humor.

Evidence suggests that babies have prenatal and womb time memories. Consequently, babies can energetically recall the feelings and emotions of their mother while in utero or during the birthing process. I would imagine how sad and vulnerable I must have been to hear my grandmother welcome me to the world in this manner. I wonder what I must of thought as a helpless little baby girl. I wonder what I said to myself in that moment, "I am unwanted," "I am unimportant," "I am unworthy," and "I must be bad."

My grandmother continued to visit us in Philadelphia a few times a year. Her visits would always start off well. We would pick her up from the 30th Street Amtrak train station (she did not fly airplanes) and we would eagerly bring her back to the house. Her short stature, wavy hair, and gentle smile would always warm my heart. Her visit would begin with us gathering around to listen to her stories about her train trip and life back home in South Georgia. The next day we would have more laughs and enjoy ourselves with several rounds of *jacks* (or 'Jack Ball' as she called it) and *Uno*. Usually by day three or four, the fussing and nagging would begin. We were instructed to clean this thing or that. She would complain that we did not do enough or help enough around the house. My grandmother was hard to please. Sometimes her comments turned to jokes and then to criticisms. My happy face turned sad because I wanted her to remain the bubbly, happy person that we picked up from the train station. I wanted her to be the grandmother who would always write me beautiful letters expressing her undying love for me. But somehow, that grandmother remained back in South Georgia.

When she sensed that she was getting on my nerves, she would call me "evil" or "mean" when I pulled away or avoided her. Sometimes at the dinner table my grandmother would say that I reminded her of a woman from her hometown named Evaline. My young ears heard '*Evil*-Leen.'

In my mind, this confirmed that my grandmother thought I was evil. I concluded that I must be indeed evil if my very own grandmother felt that way. Heck, she already called me a witch at birth. I interpreted this to mean that I was not loveable, because after all, who loves an *evil witch*? I worked hard to please her. But in my attempt to please her, I fumbled my words and made careless mistakes. My grandmother would give me a look of disappointment on a good day and sheer disgust on bad ones. It got so bad that whenever she would give me some sort of directive, my ears would seem to go deaf and I would say, "*Huh*?" This happened much too frequently for her taste. My loving grandmother would get so frustrated with me and tell me to "Stop saying 'huh' like you don't have good sense!" She would look at me as if I was the biggest idiot of all times although I know that my grandmother loved me because she told me so. Yet, I did not always feel loved by her. I did not feel good enough when she compared me to my father's side of the family or made other unkindly references about me. Looking back, I can clearly see that she was working through her own emotional pain. She was born and raised at a time when children were to be seen and not heard. Life could not have been fair to her in South Georgia during the turn of the century. I'm sure she endured unimaginable maltreatment and racism. My grandmother did the best she could for us. I have forgiven her for the hurtful things she did and said. I know that if she knew better, she would have surely done better. Rest In peace, your granddaughter loves you.

Wrong Thinking

According to the Beck Institute for Cognitive Behavioral Therapy, CBT is a psychotherapy that is based on the cognitive model. This model defines it as the way that individuals perceive a situation is more closely connected to their reaction than the situation itself. The idea is to help clients change their limited thoughts, and behavior which will result in an improved mood and overall functioning.

It has been found that people who struggle with negative thinking patterns and self-talk often catastrophize situations. This *stinking thinking* can lead to poor self-worth and confidence because you think the worst possible outcome in any given situation (eg: "It's raining today, that means I'll have a bad day!"). They blame themselves and personalize everything (eg: "Oh my god, Sharon was talking about me when she said she hates people who wear green shirts on facebook!"). They focus on the negative and filter out the good and positive things that happened (eg: "I appreciate everyone telling me all day that I did an awesome presentation, but I noticed my boss leaving the conference room for a few minutes, did she hate it?").

In the book *Self Esteem,* authors McKay and Fanning note that Psychologist Eugenia Sean call harmful thoughts the *pathological critic*. He notes that it "blames you for things that go wrong...compares you to others...sets impossible standards of perfection and then beats you up for the smallest mistakes." I call this the *Inner Critic*. The *Inner Critic* is our very own internal naysayer. It reminds us of past failures. The *Inner Critic* brings up old feelings about our abilities. It doubts our decisions. The inner critic can hold us back and debilitate us. Because of its insistent nature, most of us believe that it is indeed speaking words of truth. This is called cognitive fusion. If unproductive thoughts go unchecked, your self-esteem may suffer. Your confidence can plummet and your ability to take risks is hampered. Risks like making a career move, getting the nerve to ask someone on a date, or start a business may never be acted upon.

Hence, it can be difficult for some people to change their thoughts. A small step such as practicing gentleness when bad thoughts come can be very effective. Self- Compassion (being kind, gentle and non-judgmental to oneself) is a key tenet in Buddhism and is being practiced worldwide in many clinical settings now.

Studies show that the criticisms and demeaning put downs experienced as children from our parents, caregivers, peers and authority figures can later become our own inner voice, years after the criticisms have ceased. This inner voice can take on a life of its own. It is designed to remind us of our perceived shortcomings, limitations and insecurities. Although the inner critic can be brutal, it's intention is not malicious. The intention of the inner critical voice is to protect us from danger. It doesn't want us to fall victim to harm or an unforeseen attack. It does not want us to make a mistake or fail at a task. When it is accurate, it is useful when it helps us to recall memories such as touching hot flames will get us burned. We need the inner critic to remind us to be careful of a ferocious unleashed dog just up the road. Unfortunately, in its attempt to prevent us from 'danger,' the relentless voice in our head can go into overdrive in an attempt to help us.

Subsequently, when the inner critic is in overdrive, it can prevent important actions steps from being implemented to improve our lives. For instance, if you are considering enrolling in school to get a degree, your inner critic may say, 'you are not smart enough;' If you are thinking of a career in modeling, your inner critic might repeat 'you are not pretty enough;' If you are considering running a marathon, your inner critic might suggest that 'you are not strong enough;' If you have a desire travel to a dream location, your inner critic might say, 'you are not wealthy enough;' Or if you want to have children and start a family your inner critic may remind you that 'you are not capable enough' to accomplish your desire goals. It is apparent that the inner critic can lock us in a prison of fear, self-doubt and anxiety which can lower our self-image, self-esteem and self-confidence.

By definition, thoughts are simply an idea, notion or opinion created by thinking. Hence, thoughts shape our lives and the experiences that show up for us. What we think about, we can actually *bring* about. We can manifest or make apparent a thought held in our mind. The thought springs into action a specific set of behaviors that materialize something tangible. Your thoughts can also create an energy of movement, people and experiences to help you manifest your dreams. Thoughts can shift and change, both slowly or rapidly. We can have positive uplifting thoughts or wrong-error thinking. Thoughts are things and things can change. Thoughts are adaptable. What we think one day, we could easily be swayed to think something else the next. Thoughts can impact our mood and emotions. They can determine if we worry or feel peaceful. An unhealthy thought can produce an unhealthy behavior and vice versa. One important thing to remember about thoughts is that what we think about expands. For example, a small child scrapes her knee. If her parent reacts with fear and focus the attention on the scraped knee, the child becomes anxious and the pain may intensify. Contrarily, if you choose to think about and focus on the tranquility of taking a warm salt bath, you may start to feel relaxed and at ease. We have the power to expand our awareness and create that which brings us joy so choose your thoughts wisely!

Words Can Make You Sick

Words can uplift, encourage and support. God spoke the world into being by the power of His words (Hebrew 11:3) and Jesus reminds us that the words we speak are actually overflow of our hearts. Mother Teresa said, "kind words can be short and easy to speak, but their echoes are truly endless." Thick Nhat Hahn, a Buddhist monk in his book *Being Peace*, states "speaking honestly in any negotiation between individuals or groups is necessary. Speaking the truth in a loving way is also necessary."

As a result, what we say to ourselves internally is equally important as what we say out loud. You've heard it before, words have power! The words we speak can cut like a knife or soothe the soul of man. Words can inflict pain, hatred and violence. The use of Organ Language for example can be detrimental and could result in psychosomatic symptoms. Alfred Adler used the term "organ dialect" or "organ language" to refer to somatic (body) signs and symptoms that express attitudes or opinions. Have you ever heard yourself say, "She broke my *heart*!" How about, "You get on my *nerves*." I'm sure you've heard someone say, "He's such a pain in the *neck*!" Energetically, when you attach low vibrational words to our body parts, over time, it may actually cause physical problems so be careful what you say!

To illustrate this point, in 2004 I felt overwhelmed with financial pressures along with the responsibility of having two children under the age of 5. I would repeatedly think and say, "Oh boy, I need a vacation!" Because I felt stressed out, my resistance and immunity suffered. I had two bouts of the Flu in just over two months. Someone broke into my home and stole some of our possessions. I was exhausted and all I could think about was getting away. In January of 2004 my wish came true. My body and mind were in poor condition which allowed dis-ease to set in. I got attacked by some mysterious bacteria that was determined to wreak havoc on my body. It started off like the flu and then it evolved into thrush, muscle weakness, and breathing difficulties. My breathing became almost impossible. My blood pressure was low and my pulse was almost non-existent. My lungs collapsed and I was in big trouble. I went to the hospital alone while my husband stayed behind with our 1 ½ year old daughter and 4-year-old son. I had never been in an ambulance before nor away from my young family. I was scared. I was taken to Grady Memorial Hospital which was the best choice for the trauma my body was in. My blood was toxic and my systems were shutting down rapidly.

The hospital ran several tests, yet could not find out the source. They could not figure out the proper antibiotic that would attack the strain of bacteria my body had somehow acquired. Needless to say, I ended up with Acute Respiratory Disease and Toxic Shock Syndrome. The only choice the doctors had was to put me on a respirator and induce a coma. I was in full agreement to having a respirator because my breathing was difficult, as if trying to get air through the small hole of a straw. I witnessed people getting respirators inserted through their neck right across from me. I watched as a someone took their last breath and died in the ER near me. I left a note with my friend to take care of my children. I felt my life slipping away and knew that my world had changed. Right before going into a coma, a female resident doctor said to me, "You are very, very sick!" She went on to say sadly, "You know, you could die?" I remained in a coma for almost 21 days, away from my two small children and loving husband. I worried that my children would think I had abandoned them. What must they be think happened to me? After leaving the ER to be transferred to the ICU, the doctors eventually met with my husband to tell him to start making funeral plans. *Funeral Plans*?!? My husband, siblings, family, and close friends could not believe what they were hearing or witnessing. This was unfathomable! They were perplexed about how a "healthy person" could get so sick. They wanted answers and they never let go of hope for my full recover. My family and friends did what they could to heal me. My closest friends and former co-workers came to see me in the hospital. My siblings and in-laws flew here from up north to see about me and to help fight for my life.

My family and friends come from a diverse background of faiths and spiritual practices such as Christianity, Ifa, Yoruba, Akan, Islam, and Kemetic traditions. Each one did what they needed to do to help me during my health crisis. Some created prayer circles and fasted on my behalf. Some set up altars. Others did rituals to include sending healing light my way. Someone danced in a healing circle in African. Pictures were put up at my bedside to remind me of my family. Candles were lit on my behalf. Some surrounded my hospital bed and prayed like never before. Some held a vision for my full recovery. I was in a circle of love.

While in my coma I had many surreal experiences, some in which I will not share now. However, I had visions, sensations and epiphanies while in the coma. An overwhelming *pull* to be with my parents (both deceased) had a stronghold on me. I wanted desperately to be with them again. I had lapses in my memory that had me to believe that I did not have children to care for. I did not realize that I had people who loved and needed me back on earth. My mind could not recall such important details. A grainy vision of a group of *Elders* or *Ancestors* came into view. At that moment, I experienced an overwhelming feeling of love. With great reverence and humility, I asked them to allow me to rejoin my family. A wave of the most beautiful resounding feeling of "YES" came over me and I was granted the permission I sought. The prayers, chants, affirmations, visioning and declarations over my life broke through my temporary illusions. My reality returned and became clear that I had a loving husband, two beautiful children, siblings and friends who loved me and needed me here.

My eyes opened shortly thereafter to see my husband's long-awaited smile, which seemed like the most beautiful sight I had ever seen. The next day my precious children came to see me and my heart just opened with pure joy. Seeing my babies again was the best gift I could ever ask for. The resident doctor who said that I could have died came to me and cried. She told me that she was very concerned for me and did not think that I would make it. Although she meant well, I'm glad I did not believe her and I forgave her.

Prior to this, all I wanted was to have a vacation. I said it and thought about it daily. My vacation came did it not? It was not the vacation I had desired but it was the vacation that I had created. When we ask for what we want our emotions and vibration must be high and positive, not low and negative. To help your desires, you must think it, speak it, feel it (with positive emotions), know it and then be in gratitude for it. I am blessed to be here to practice what I now know. I am careful to speak *life* into my life!!!

A key point to note is that words should never be used to harm anyone or invoke fear in someone. Sometimes knowing how to use words to reveal what we desire can be intimidating and scary. I am mindful of using my words in positive ways. When I forget, I immediately say or think "cancel" to erase what was said. My daily affirmations have landed me jobs and opportunities. I have spoken into existence health and healing for me and my family. Substantial amounts of money have shown up in what seemed like impossible odds. Legal issues were resolved with no consequence. It's more than a cliché, words really do have power!

The Mind Can Heal the Body

When I was a child mother used to always say 'Mind over Matter' whenever we thought we could not achieve something. She would try to convince me that what we conceive and believe, we can achieve. Early on, she understood the power of the mind. My mother understood that it is possible to control physical conditions using the mind. But for me I didn't buy into my mother's notion about the mind having power over my experience. It just didn't seem real to me. One day,

I experienced the most horrific headache ever experienced in my young life. Having an intense pain in my head was foreign to me. I found myself in a state of misery, feeling debilitated by this strange pain. One thing was for sure, I never wanted to feel this pain again. At the tender age of 9, I decided to experiment with my mother's 'Mind over Matter' concept and began to imagine every day that I was "free of headaches." I declared that I would not have headaches. I told everyone I knew that "I didn't get headaches." I said it so much that I began to believe it. Not only did I believe it, I felt it in my bones. I did not have another headache for 35 years! I was headache-free because I changed my thinking, used words as a tool to manifest my desired outcome, and used the power of the Subconscious Mind to manifest my desires.

According to Canadian Neuropsychologists Donald Hebb, known for his work in the field of associative learning said, "Neurons that fire together wire together." What that means is that everything that we think, feel, and experience triggers thousands of neurons that form a type of neural network in our brains. Repeating, thinking or believing something over and over, our brains learn to trigger the same neurons each time. Even at 9 years old, I was creating new neural connections and associations. Unbeknownst to me, I was rewiring my brain! This sparked my interest and I became intrigued with the concept of mind over matter.

Hypnotherapy as a Healing Method

Many years later I traveled with a colleague/friend to a conference on substance abuse in Savannah, Georgia around 2012. As most conferences tend to be, this one was long and drawn out and I felt restless and bored. Suddenly one of the speakers lectured about helping addicted clients using hypnotherapy. Hearing this *new* method to help clients sparked my interests. I was no longer bored. I leaned in with anticipation of the next piece of data the speaker shared. The prospect of acquiring a skillset that can use the power of the mind for change was exciting. This changed my professional and personal life forever! My mind was blown wide open with anticipation of my new journey.

Soon after the conference, I researched this technique and the many ways it could support clients in their healing journey. In my quest for knowledge, I came upon an article that led me to an African American hypnotherapist in New York. I contacted her by phone and we immediately hit it off. After a 2-hour conversation I was inspired by her beautiful spirit, extensive knowledge and her successful Manhattan hypnotherapy practice. With her help, I decided to pursue my desire to be a hypnotherapist. Shortly thereafter I found myself packing my bags for New Mexico to begin my extensive training in hypnotherapy. When I arrived in Albuquerque I immediately felt connected to my new 'tribe' of helpers and healers. I was enthralled with the conversations and the energy that these 'healers' exuded. My time in New Mexico was life altering, filled with deep and meaningful lessons of transformational work.

Hypnosis uses the subconscious mind to effect change. Isn't that what my mother had been trying to teach me all along? As you are reading this, you are in your conscious level of awareness. You are consciously able to make your own decisions, reason and use your logic to accomplish tasks. You are most likely using all your senses and your deductive and inductive reasoning capabilities are in full effect. Within your conscious mind is a mechanism referred to as the critical faculty. According to Tim Simmerman in *Medical Hypnotherapy,* the critical facility acts like a gatekeeper or filtering mechanism to the subconscious mind. Its job is to determine if new information or a new situation (i.e., a job interview) matches or is congruent with the past programming of the subconscious mind ("I never get the job"). Hypnotherapy helps to relax the critical faculty which then allows the conscious and the subconscious mind to talk to one another. When they are able to communicate, it is easier to shift your attention to and accept healthier suggestions without having to pass through the processing go the conscious mind ("My interviewing skills have improved and I just might get this job!").

The subconscious mind is literal and does not know the difference between reality and fantasy. The subconscious mind is a level of consciousness that records everything from our past, right up to our present moment. These recordings of perceived current or past fears and anxiety stimulate our Sympathetic Nervous System (SNS) to activate the release of hormones into our bloodstream that increase our heart rate, breathing and dilates our pupils. The role of the Sympathetic Nervous System is to create the *fight or flight* response to protect us from perceived danger.

Hypnosis done by a qualified hypnotherapist can help you enter your Parasympathetic Nervous System (PNS), your *rest and digest* response. Your PNS slows down your heart rate, moderates breathing, improves digestion and create homeostasis. In this state, you are able to receive new and helpful information to disrupt and reverse the negative programming of the past. In this state, you are able to embrace positive thoughts and ideas that are more in line with your true self, your *higher* self. Some believe that this deep understanding of your inner power, strengthens the connection between you and the Creator of the Universe.

Hypnosis and Religion

My belief is that we are all spiritual beings, having physical and emotional experiences on planet earth. I believe that we are born with a divine intelligence and a higher self that connects us to our spiritual Source. Understanding and adhering to Universal Laws guides my life and my work as a psychotherapist and hypnotherapist. Working with individuals to help them feel better through the transformation of their minds is my life's calling. I love what I do and look forward to working with clients who are striving to discover their inner wisdom, strength and power. Although my understanding of spirituality may be different from my client's, I believe that all of humans are spiritually connected and that we desire to be our best, feel accepted, and to be loved.

Moreover, several of my clients shared with me that hypnotherapy helped to open their hearts and heightened their sense of awareness. Subsequently, a renewed spiritual awakening or connection occurred as a result of our work together.

Hypnotherapy is not for everyone. In fact, some of my Christian clients are apprehensive about this treatment. In the past when I would be invited to speak at churches, many people turned away in fear and skepticism. We discussed this resistance during my training and so I was prepared for the skeptics, or so I thought. I continued to be taken aback by the responses and reactions by some (not all Christians reacted this way). People said things like, "Where is Jesus in this?" Or "My Pastor told me to never get hypnotized!" or "Is this Voodoo?"

A former client who was making great progress told me how she felt "empowered" after our sessions. However, the client later shared that another counselor (who happened to be Christian) told her to be careful of "demon spirits" while in hypnosis. Even though the client had improved immensely over the months in treatment, the thought of demon spirits scared her and she never returned. This could have crushed my spirit. However, I personally and professionally witnessed the healing power of this technique, I could not be deterred. As with any method, hypnotherapy is not perfect and I am not professing that it should be a panacea for all troubles and problems. In fact, no therapeutic intervention is 100% effective.

Some of my clients have chosen not to use this technique and that choice is absolutely fine. I would never pressure anyone to do anything they wish not to do. That would be unethical, immoral, and unprofessional. As a professional psychotherapist and hypnotherapist, it does not matter what religion my client practices because I have a sense of spiritual oneness and connectedness that transcends religious differences. My only job is to hold the vision of wellness and to *see* the pure potential of my clients.

Slaying the Inner Critic

What I know for sure is that we should be mindful of our thoughts because thoughts evoke emotions. Emotions are energy in motion. Energy flows where your attention goes. Simply put your energy on the things you desire rather than the things you don't.

Perhaps, *slaying* the inner critic is not what I actually want you to do. Slaying something sounds brutal and hostile. It does not promote a good image or productive feeling. The idea of slaying something sounds and feels harsh and unforgiving. In fact, the inner critic was developed because of harsh words or treatment you received. Now that you have the capacity to think, speak and feel on a higher vibration, you can now offer the inner critic your understanding and compassion to transform it.

A key step to transforming your inner critic is to take away its credibility. With just a little bit of curiosity, you are likely to discover sufficient evidence to discredit your negative beliefs. You might discover that your inner critical voice is not grounded in truth and in many cases far from accurate. Remember that the act of having thoughts does not make them true. Thoughts are not always factual. You might have *thought* that your husband was cheating on you with your fiend only to find out that they were secretly planning your surprise birthday party. Just knowing that your thoughts could be wrong is a revolutionary breakthrough.

Transforming the inner critic is an ongoing journey. It is a layered approach to include acknowledging the negative thoughts, that inevitably show up, yet allowing them to pass through without judgement. Offer yourself compassion when you over react or condemn yourself. Forgive yourself for thinking the negative thought in the first place. Focus on your personal victories and triumphs instead of fixating on your failures and shortcoming. Removing the inner critic will help you start viewing the cup *half full* instead of *half empty*. It will allow you to imagine a world full of amazing possibilities.

Not only is it imperative to change the way we speak and think we must also take care of our bodies with good nutrition, exercise and water intake. I believe that filling our cup spiritually is equally as important to our total wellness and wholeness. This process may take many forms such as going to church, attending Mosque, connecting with nature, going to an Ashram, doing prayer work, meditation or whatever connects you to Divine Spirit.

In summary, I get excited when helping my clients eliminate the inner critic and destroy the mental 'prison' they have built from the bricks self-limiting thinking. My holistic approach (mind, body and spirit) helps them to heal the wounded inner critic and transform it into an *Inner Coach*. Instead of the nasty little inner critic, the Inner Coach is encouraging, compassionate and understanding. The Inner Coach rebuilds confidence, courage and self-worth. Its' role is to remind you of the divine truth about who you are. The simple truth is that you are whole, perfect and complete.

References:

- Patrick Fanning and Mathew McKay, PHD, *Self Esteem.*

- Joseph Murphy, Ph.D., D.D, *The Power of Your Subconscious Mind.*

- Tim Simmerman Sierra, *Medical Hypnotherapy Volume One.*

- Catherine M. Pittman, PHD and Elizabeth M.Karle, MLIS, *Rewire Your Anxious Brain.*

- John Court, Professor of Psychology, University of South Australia Ph.D., Clinical Psychology, University of Adelaide Diploma of Clinical Hypnosis, Australian Society of Hypnosis Certificate in Theology, Sydney
- Paul Durbin, United Methodist minister Chaplain (Brigadier General), United States Army (retired 1989) Director of Pastoral Care & Clinical Hypnotherapy, Methodist Hospital, New Orleans, LA (retired 2001) Director of Clinical Hypnotherapy, MHSF, affiliated with Methodist Hospital (retired June 30, 2005).

What You Need to Know About Hypnotherapy

Gena Golden, LCSW

Hypnosis and Hypnotherapy can be very successful in treating people for a wide range of conditions such as confidence, self-esteem, test anxiety, weight loss, stop smoking, nail biting, stress reduction and phobias etc. Hypnotherapy is the use of hypnosis for therapeutic healing by a trained and qualified professional. Hypnosis is a natural, yet altered state of mind, where the critical factor of the conscious mind is relaxed and selective thinking is maintained. Selective thinking, or focused concentration, is the ability to rest your mind on a selected idea. When the critical factor is relaxed through hypnosis, communication between the conscious and the subconscious mind is possible for change. It's important to note that all Hypnosis is Self-Hypnosis. This is great news because it shows that the power is within you. It also means that you have control. We each have the power to hypnotize ourselves for the purposes of clarity, calm and healing.

History of Hypnosis

The term hypnosis is derived from the Greek word hypnos, meaning sleep. The origin of modern Western hypnotherapy is often traced to the Austrian physician Franz Anton Mesmer (1734-1815). Mesmer believed that illness is caused by an imbalance of magnetic fluids in the body that can be corrected through "animal magnetism." He asserted that the hypnotist's own personal magnetism can be transferred to a patient. The term "mesmerize" is derived from Mesmer's name.

Various forms of hypnosis, trance, and altered states of consciousness have been documented in several cultures throughout history. Hypnosis-like practices can be traced to ancient

Egypt, Babylon, Greece, Persia, Britain, Scandinavia, America, Africa, India, and China. Wong Tai, a father of Chinese medicine, made an early written reference to hypnosis in 2600 BC. Hypnotic practices have played roles in religion and religious ceremonies. It is mentioned in the Bible, Talmud, and Hindu Vedas, and trance-states are included in some Native American and African ceremonies.

Sleep temples (also known as dream temples or Egyptian sleep temples) are regarded by some as an early instance of hypnosis over 4000 years ago, under the influence of Imhotep. Imhotep served as Chancellor, and High Priest of the sun god Ra at Heliopolis. He was said to be a son of Ptah, his mother being a mortal named Khredu-ankh. Sleep temples were hospitals of sorts, healing a variety of ailments, perhaps many of them psychological in nature. The treatment involved chanting, placing the patient into a trance-like or hypnotic state, and analyzing their dreams in order to determine treatment. Meditation, fasting, baths and sacrifices to the patron deity or other spirits were often involved as well. Sleep temples also existed in the Middle East and Ancient Greece.

In Greece, they were built in honor of Asclepios, the Greek God of Medicine and were called Asclepieion. The Greek treatment was referred to as incubation, and focused on prayers to Asclepios for healing. A similar Hebrew treatment was referred to as Kavanah, and involved focusing on letters of the Hebrew alphabet spelling the name of the Hebrew God. Sir Mortimer Wheeler unearthed a Roman Sleep temple at Lydney Park, Gloucestershire in 1928, with the assistance of a young J.R.R. Tolkien.

As you can see, hypnosis is not a new practice at all. In fact, various forms of hypnosis have been around for hundreds of years practiced by various cultures and religious groups. You may have already hypnotized yourself and did not know it.

Today, hypnosis is used with much more care and consideration to the client. There are informed consents and HIPAA rules to follow. Confidentiality and proper touch must to implement always. Qualified hypnotherapists are often psychologist, licensed counselors or clinical social workers. It's important to find a hypnotist that is also a mental health professional to ensure proper training, safety and confidentiality.

I utilize hypnotherapy in ways that support my clients in uncovering, or discovering for the first time, their innate abilities. It is the client who heals herself. I simply travel with them on their journey, guiding them along the way.

Hypnotherapy can be mixed with other modalities such as CBT (Cognitive Behavioral Therapy, Solution Focused, Mindfulness, Gestalt) and the like for more effectiveness. This eclectic approach is what I use to transform the negative self-limiting thinking and behavioral patterns that keep clients stuck in bad relationships, stagnated in their prospective careers and mired in low self-confidence. It is my job to help them to recognize patterns of self-sabotage that create an unhappy life and then explore new ways to break the vicious cycle of emotional pain and discomfort. Through this process of self-discovery, my clients come away with an understanding that they have the power to reframe and challenge thoughts and behaviors to get the results they desire in their lives.

Christian Concerns about Hypnotherapy

Many of my Christian clients struggle with seeking help from a mental health professional as a whole. Some of the messages they receive from family and church members including discouragement from seeking help outside of the church. Additionally, there may be an implication toward a sense of "wrongness" or innuendo that going to a counselor is "unGodly". According to an article on the **Hypnosis Network,** '*Christianity and Hypnosis: Answers from an Academic and a Minister',* John Court, Professor of Psychology, University of South Australia Ph.D., Clinical Psychology responds to questions about why some Christians are concerned that by undergoing hypnosis they might be going against their faith. Court responds,

> "Because they have been told, or have read in Christian books, that hypnosis is condemned in the Bible. Those who love to find a proof text for their beliefs use one word in Deuteronomy 18 (vv 10-11). In English, the Hebrew word is usually translated 'charmer,' or 'one who casts spells,' and from other contexts it is clear that the word refers to snake charming. To relate it to hypnosis is quite misleading. Good exegesis, of course, calls for more than a simple proof text, and this is lacking. On the other hand, there are two examples in the Acts where it refers to Peter going into a trance (the Greek word is ekstasis from which we get 'ecstasy') and both events are reported as both positive and significant."

Court goes on to explain why Christians should not have a problem with trying hypnosis by stating, ".... They have been told Christians must not be hypnotized because that would be to relinquish their free will to another person. If that view can be shown to be false, then it is possible to proceed. I am saddened at how many Christian people feel unable to accept hypnotic-based interventions, when they could be very helpful in dealing with physical and emotional issues. Christians will also often report with surprise that the experience is spiritually beneficial, as it is possible to incorporate prayer and meditation into the therapeutic process."

According to Paul Durbin, United Methodist Minister and Director of Pastoral Care & Clinical Hypnotherapy:

> "Each one here comes with his/her own history: religiously, personally, and professionally. I come to you as a Christian Minister who looks upon hypnosis as a valuable tool of counseling. Coming from a religious profession and working in a church related hospital for 30 years, I was often asked, "Why does one of religious faith need hypnosis?" or "How can you use hypnosis? Isn't there a conflict between religious faith and hypnosis?" I believe that these questions can be responded to by referring to the statement of Jesus in John 10:10, "I am come that they may have life and have it more abundantly." Hypnosis is one of the gifts of God which help people experience the "more abundant life." Hypnosis is neither anti-religious nor pro-religious. It can be used for good or bad depending on the hypnotist and the subject. Today, most religious groups accept the proper ethical use of hypnosis for helping people. The Roman Catholic Church has issued statements approving the use of hypnosis. In 1847, a decree from the Sacred Congregation of The Holy Office stated, "Having removed all misconceptions, foretelling of the future, explicit or implicit invocation of the devil, the use hypnosis is indeed merely an act of making use of physical media that are otherwise licit and hence it is not morally forbidden provided it does not tend toward an illicit end or toward anything depraved."

Myths about Hypnotherapy

There are many myths out there, so I understand if you are a little concerned about being hypnotized. Hollywood, for example, continues to depict stage hypnotist as having the power to make someone do what they simply do not want to do. I'm sure you've seen people quacking like a duck, barking like a dog or participating in other silly or foolish acts at the expense of the 'subject'. The movie,'Get Out' further perpetuates the depiction of false stereotypes of hypnotherapists taking *control* of one's mind. While entertaining, this is incorrect. People of color, in particular, tend to be skeptical mostly due to history of being misled, misdiagnosed and untreated by medical professionals. In high school, we learned about some of the infamous clinical studies conducted by the U.S. Public Health Service to include the Tuskegee Syphilis Experiment and the story about Henrietta Lacks, an African American woman whose cancer cells were the source of the HeLa cell line, the first immortalized cell line and one of the most important cell lines in medical research. Although not targeted to people of color the MK Ultra aka CIA Mind Control Project which conducted covert tests including subjecting the unwitting subjects to hallucinogenic drugs and other chemicals. I understand the trepidation when it comes to allowing someone to work on the mind. I don't blame them. So, for me, taking the time to educate people helps to make them feel comfortable. I explain that the power is within them and that they will remain in control at all times. Below are a few common Myths that I address with my clients and people in the community that are interested: **Myth #1 "It's Mind Control".** Myth Buster: Hypnotherapy is not mind control. If anyone can control your mind, it's you! Hypnotherapy does not control your mind; it only relaxes you to be more open and receptive to positive suggestions and imagery to reach your personal goals. The hypnotherapist is always checking in with you and doesn't do or say anything that doesn't feel right to you. **Myth #2 "I can get 'stuck' in hypnosis."** Myth Buster: No one has ever gotten stuck in hypnosis. You can stop at any time you like. Even if left alone, your natural response will be to awaken. In hypnosis clients tend to be hyper-aware as your senses are sharpened. **Myth #3 "I will be made a fool of myself!"** Myth Buster: Your ego is always intact and so although you will be in deeply relaxed hypnotic state, you are aware and can choose what you will or will not do. Hypnotherapy is a method used to help you heal, grow and accomplish your goals, it's not to make you feel foolish or out of control. **Myth #4 "Hypnosis is a truth serum."** Myth Buster: Even in hypnosis, you have a choice of what you share or not share. You cannot be 'made' to say or share what you don't want to. **Myth #5 "I'm too strong willed, in control of my mind, and too intelligent to be hypnotized."** Myth Buster:

Remember that hypnosis is natural. We all experience a hypnotic state every day when we drive home from work or school and don't know how we got there; or when an athlete gets in the 'zone' when playing a sport; or when we day dream but are still aware of everything going on around us. Strong willed, controlled and intelligent people are ideal for hypnotherapy because they are highly creative, imaginative and have the ability to use focused attention to get results fast.

Questions to ask a Hypnotherapist

Hypnosis is a safe and pleasant experience when used correctly. Hypnotherapists will employ a variety of styles to help you achieve your goal. Many celebrities and elite athletes have hired Hypnotherapists to help them overcome anxieties, improve their performance and lose weight (just to name a few). Here are questions to help you find the right Hypnotherapist for you.

1. Do you offer a free consultation?

2. Can you show me evidence of your personal results?

3. Do you offer support between sessions? If so what kind?

4. Have you had a recognized training or certification?

5. Are you insured?

6. Are you taking any medication yourself as it's important I work with someone who isn't potentially suffering from what I am suffering from?

7. What tools do you offer such as CD's or MP3's?

8. What is the minimum and maximum amount of sessions for my problem?

9. How qualified are you for treating my condition?

10. What ongoing training do you have?

11. Who is your ideal client?

12. What conditions are you less good at treating?

13. How will you protect me during Hypnosis?

14. How can you reassure me that I will always be in control during Hypnosis?

15. Do you offer a follow up service?

16. What are the reasons why I should select you?

17. Are you also a licensed mental health professional (psychologist, psychiatrist, social worker, counselor or therapist)?

First Session:

The first session involves you sharing information about yourself, your past coping mechanisms, your desire for change, and your stated goals for the treatment. There may be a host of questions to answer to help the hypnotherapist understand the problem. The hypnotherapist may then educate you about the levels of the mind, various states of consciousness, what happens to the body in trance state and answer any questions that you may have. It will also be determined at this session, the length, duration and frequency of the sessions. The cost or fees associated with the treatment will be determined as well. Your expectations and questions will also be explored throughout treatment.

The hypnotherapist may not do hypnosis with you until the second, third or sometimes fourth session to establish a solid rapport with you. This is important that you to feel safe and secure while in hypnosis. This also helps the hypnotherapist to understand your struggles, triggers and history for effective treatment. Your hypnotherapist is also establishing your emotionalized desire to change as this is key to your success.

Most Hypnotherapists will welcome questions and engage with you in dialogue via phone or in person, as they understand that finding the right practitioner is important for you. Once you've found the ideal Hypnotherapist, enjoy the wonderful benefits Hypnotherapy can bring.

Anxiety Disorder

Demetria Hill Cannady, PhD, LPC

Anxiety is defined as a feeling of worry, nervousness, or unease, typically about an imminent event or something with an uncertain outcome; desire to do something typically accompanied with unease; a nervous disorder characterized by a state of excessive uneasiness and apprehension, typically with compulsive behavior or panic attacks (www.Merriam-WebsterDictionary.com). Anxiety Disorder is caused by feelings or excessive worry, nervousness, and being tense about events which may or may not have occurred. Anxiety generally causes one to experience irrational fears about the events. You find yourself being unable to control the worry you experience about events such as day-to-day events, natural disasters, health, finances, your children/ parents, and school/work.

The DSM-V describes Anxiety as Generalized Anxiety Disorder as the following: The presence of excessive worry about a variety of topics, events, or activities. Worry occurs more often than not for at least six months and is clearly excessive. There are six symptoms that are present within Generalized Anxiety Disorder for more days than not for the past six months: restlessness and feelings of being on edge; being easily fatigued; difficulty concentrating; irritability; muscle tension; and sleep disturbance. The anxiety, worry, or physical symptoms cause clinically significant distress or impairment in social, occupational, or important areas of functioning (American Psychiatric Association, 2013).

There are is about nineteen percent of American which experience anxieties so having anxiety related issues does not make you abnormal. However, there are strategies which one may try to reduce and/or overcome anxieties which are frequently occurring:

Self-evaluate how the anxieties affect you. Are your thoughts rational or irrational about the event(s)? Most often the thoughts are irrational thus throwing us in an exaggerated state of worry. Do not worry about those things which you have not control of. My favorite saying is "Pray about it." If you choose to worry about it then don't pray about it. If you have prayed about it, release it to God and allow him to do His work.

Set up structure; relinquish control; revise your reactions; trust yourself; practice yoga; laugh at your thoughts (irrational); you need to be able to differentiate between fact and fiction; and stop attempting to please everyone. If you're pleased with your event and outcome this is the most important, especially if you've done your best. Utilizing some or all these techniques will allow you to decrease anxiety attacks.

American Psychiatric Association, (2013). Diagnostic and statistical manual of mental disorders, 5th Ed. Washington, DC.

 Wanda Major Thomas is a retail sales retiree from J.C. Penney and Belk in Thomasville, GA of over 25 years. She has also worked as a waitress, hostess, seamstress, secretary, photographer, and personal care nurse. She enjoyed every job as each added another dimension to her level of learning life's lessons.

After over 9 years of research, Wanda has just finished completed her first book, "The Long Journey Back- A Major Family History Part 1." A compilation of family documents such as censuses and tax records, marriage and death certificates, along with short introductions for great, great aunts and uncles. She has answered many questions that puzzled family members for decades.

She is an active Jehovah's Witness that volunteers as part of a worldwide preaching work, sharing good news about God's Kingdom (Matt 6:9,10). Wanda spends an average of 150 to 200 hours per year as she enjoys speaking with others about God's promise for the earth.

She is married to William Thomas, the mother of one daughter, Demetria Hill Cannady, grandmother of five grandchildren, and a friend to many. In her spare time, she enjoys spending time with family (sometimes hard to do), doing genealogical research, working in her flowers, and learning to make candles.

MY PERSONAL QUEST FOR BIBLE TRUTH

WANDA M. THOMAS

"The truth shall set you free!!" The pastor thundered those words from the pulpit. As a child, I wanted to know what I would be free from. Statements such as: "Repent and you shall be saved." "Good people go to heaven." And "If you're bad, you're going to go to hell and burn forever in a hell fire." I was intrigued by the prospect of someone being so bad that God would torment them for ever and ever in a hell fire. However, I was afraid that I could be one of those who would get sent to hell. I tried to be "good" and at times I worked really hard to be good only to do something that I knew God did not like. Then I would pray, pray, pray. I prayed for all kinds of things because I had been taught that God answers prayers. I prayed for more money, a better house, a new house, a car, bigger legs, more clothes, better grades...anything that I felt I should ask God for because He could give it to me. Different ones in the family would get sick and I would pray for them to get better. When they did, I'd figure God did answer my prayers and those other things didn't really matter, because I didn't get them. At some point, I wondered who I was really praying to because I didn't understand how Jesus could be God and God be Jesus, especially since Jesus had stated that "he had been sent to do his father's will." How could the one being sent decide to do what he wanted instead of what he was told to do? I just really didn't understand it.

Sunday mornings were so much fun as we all scrambled to get dressed. Saturday night was when we would get our clothes ready for Sunday. When morning came, I would help get the boys (my brothers) ready first. It was funny thinking back on how they would squirm because of having to sit still until time to go. Many times, we walked to church in order to get there for Sunday

School. If we only had Sunday School, which was held every Sunday, we would walk back home, walking down the railroad tracks, putting our ears down on the track to listen for a train that might be coming our way. I can remember seeing only one train during all those years. Boy, we jumped up and down, counting cars until we were tired! We stopped by the drug store to spend any money that we had not put into the collection plate. Then we ate our goodies as we ambled along. On the second and fourth Sundays, the adults came later for our regular church service. After church, we would all pile into the car and head home to a wonderful Sunday dinner. Those were some of the best times of my life as we gathered together afterwards at Grandma and Granddaddy's house. Sometimes all the families and cousins would come and stay late into the night. We played every game that we could think of. The older children acted older, sitting around laughing and talking quietly about boyfriends and girlfriends. We loved it when our cousins from other states came home. It was especially special! As I grew older, I joined the older cousins in their conversations.

Our church, much like other churches met twice a month, second and fourth Sundays. We, children, all joined the church and got baptized when we were young. This was our protection for when we weren't so good. We all joined the Jr. Choir and I joined the Usher Board. Sometimes there were special meetings and these were special days that bring back fond memories of a time when everything was good. There were guest ministers and others from various churches that fellowshipped with us. All seemed good.

Of course, we had the usual celebrations, church anniversary, men's day, women's day, and most importantly, the preacher's anniversary. These were always money-making events as we reached deep into our purses and wallets. I wondered what happened to "You received free, give free." On special occasions, we were given brown envelopes in which to put our tithes. I remember how hard it was our family of eight, always giving more than we had.

Once a year, there was a "turnout". This was almost like a small festival that everyone attended with the emphasis being on " having a good time." All in the community came and ate. The ladies in the church at Trinity and other churches spent much time preparing picnic baskets filled to the top with wonderful foods. There were a variety of rice, stews, vegetables of all sorts, breads - homemade and bought and of course; everyone's favorite - **Fried chicken**! Cakes, pies and cobblers topped the day off and in the end, it seemed that we brought back as much food as we had taken. There was a barrel bought just for making lemonade, enough to give five gallons or more to anyone to take home. Hand-squeezed lemons and lots of sugar mixed with love equaled the best tasting lemonade ever made!! Oh! What a glorious time we all had! Everyone left happy, full and satisfied. Memories such as these made me proud to be a part of that church.

But, as time went by, the church drifted away from what was the norm and begin to follow the ways of the churches that were 'more modern and up to date.' In order to be more modern, they needed more money and this posed a problem. No one really had any more than they had before so this called for more money-making ventures.

On one of those occasions while attending a different church in adulthood, all the women and girls were supposed to give specific amounts of fifty and twenty-five dollars. There was a woman who had four daughters and she was supposed to give one hundred fifty dollars for the five of them. However, she was very, very poor. As a result, she didn't have *any* amount to give. The women's day program started and soon the names were being called off the sheet along with the amount in the envelopes. The names rolled off the list - one by one - Sister Pearl E.- $50.00, Sister Edna E. - $50.00 ... Then he started - Sister Sarah R. - 0, Sister Elaine R. - 0, Sister Mary R. - 0, Sister Leslie R.- 0, Sister Rhonda R.- 0. I was horrified as I listened! Finally, the agony was over.

After the program, everyone met in the annex to eat but Mrs. R. wasn't there. I went out back and there she sat with her head in her hands, crying her heart out. I went over to her and asked her what was wrong. She continued to cry as she related how sad and embarrassed she was. It upset me to see her so upset, so I lit up a cigarette and tried to comfort and encourage her. She was sad because of not having the money for the program but embarrassed because of her name and the children's names being called out loud. She felt that they could have just not called their names at all. That moment has remained with me until this day, reminding me of that sinking feeling of despair that she must have felt. Many months passed and I did not see her or her children again. When I finally saw her again, she stated that she just did not have the 'heart to come back to that church any time soon.'

As I grew older, I read the Bible almost daily but didn't understand much of what I was reading. I loved the Bible and many of the books drew me in and fascinated me. The book of Genesis spoke of a beautiful garden that Adam and Eve lost. It told the story of the Nephilim...amazing giants that were bullies. The Tower of Babel and how God confused the languages of the people helped me to understand how we got some of our languages and other religions. A little further into the book it tells the end result of how God felt and still feels about homosexuality. The Bible told of success and failure, it told of love and hate, blessings and maledictions. However, at the end, it spoke of a river and trees for healing the nations. How I longed for that time to come.

I was a child with a vivid imagination and as a result, the book of Revelation scared me with the vivid descriptions of wild beasts, some having ten horns and seven heads. Still I read about these beasts but didn't understand their significance. The book of Revelation at verse three starts with the words: "Happy is the one who reads aloud and those who hear the words of this prophecy and who observe the things written in it..." I wondered how anyone could possibly be 'happy' while reading this book. However, I came to understand that this is a book written with many descriptions of beasts to represent world powers that have come and gone. And to encourage all to remain faithful to the end regardless of all the things that will take place. The end could be the end of our lives or the end of this world as we know it now, with its violence, hatred, and disregard for many of its many wonderful blessings. It gives us a prophetic look at world governments and their effect on mankind and what will eventually happen to them; resulting in happiness for all of mankind.

I was always amazed at the different statements made by the pastor and often could not follow his line of logic. Many of the scriptures that were read left me with more questions than answers. As I soon discovered though, there were no answers to the questions I asked from the people I asked.

At age 16, I decided to search for some answers that made sense, not according to the preacher but according to the Bible. I decided to search out different religions to get a better understanding of what others believed and to ascertain which teachings kept close to what the Bible taught. It was quite a search, talking to other Baptists, the Mormons, Seventh Day Adventists, Catholics, Church of Christ, Muslims and others. One of the others was the Hare Krishna movement. I didn't know it was a form of Hinduism, worshiping the god Krishna. This one wasn't for me. The information was exciting as I worked to piece together what paralleled with the Bible's teachings and compared them with what I had already been taught.

At age 17, I was quite excited as I visited the public library in Atlanta, Georgia and found that there were hundreds of books on religion. I spent hours upon hours in that library. It was so amazing to be able to read about any religion that was known to me as well as others that I had not known such as Lutheranism, Calvinism, Taoism, and Buddhism. I tried to understand what it meant to worship something or someone other than God. It was difficult.

Sometime later, I met a man, married and had one child. It was during this period that I had my first initial personal contact with Jehovah's Witnesses. Time came and went and I found myself divorced with a child. Working and caring for a young child was quite daunting as I tried to do a balancing act. Times were difficult but not so difficult that I wanted to move back home. I prayed constantly for strength and guidance as there were days that I didn't feel like getting out of bed. I knew that God had a personal name because I remembered that as a child, Jehovah's Witnesses had often visited my mother and she had studied with them for some time. They used the scripture at Psalm 83:18 and Exodus 6:3 to show her God's personal name. She had a beautiful book titled: **"From Paradise Lost to Paradise Regained"**. This book intrigued me as it depicted the beautiful paradise that Adam and Eve had lost. I looked at the pictures and read page after page of mankind's problems but eventually a cure for all the problems. That book was my first real contact with the truth about what had truly happened to man. But it offered hope beyond the present problems. My mind turned to the pages of that book when days were especially hectic. From Paradise Lost to Paradise Regained became an anchor for my hope in Jehovah and the promises that He had made. It helped me through a divorce and being a single parent. I dreamed of a paradise where my child, my grandchildren, other relatives and I would live each and every day without anything bad happening ever again. I felt that those promises had been made to me personally.

Eventually, I met two Jehovah's Witnesses as stated earlier. At first, I watched as they came to the door and knocked, then they left. I felt a little bad at first, but eventually that feeling went away. I reasoned that I had just put my daughter to sleep and all that talking might wake her up. They went to all the doors and knocked and talked to those that answered. A few weeks later, they were back in our apartment complex again. I wondered...how could they just go up to a total stranger's house without being invited and then talk to someone about the Bible. I knew...that wasn't for me.

I, apparently had not been paying attention because when they knocked, it startled me. My first impulse was to ignore them again but something pushed me toward the door. I opened the door and they introduced themselves and told me that they were in the neighborhood. I can't remember exactly what they said but whatever it was, I jumped at the opportunity to "set them straight." And although I knew next to less than nothing about their religion, I had an idea. I figured that I would ask them a few questions and send them on their way. My first questions were, "What holidays do you'll celebrate? Do you celebrate Christmas?" I latched on to Jeremiah 10:1-5, equating that with celebrating Christmas. They told me that Jehovah's Witnesses do not celebrate any holidays. The only worldwide celebration that they took part in was the memorial of Jesus Christ's death. This takes place every year on the date that corresponds with Nisan 14, on the Jewish calendar, the date that Jesus Christ was put to death. This is always a few days before

Easter. Thirty minutes later we were still talking and that led to them saying that they would be back the next week.

Consequently, I began to study the Bible with Jehovah's Witnesses and I started a study in the book, **"The truth that leads to everlasting life."** I did attend a few meetings. They loved my daughter and thought that she "was the cutest little thing!" Everyone was so nice that I didn't believe it! They didn't ask me to stand up and say my name or anything like that. That was a surprise. But the biggest surprise was - there was no collection plate ever passed! Not once! There was no choir - I was told that Jehovah wanted everyone to sing and praise Him. Everyone used their Bibles and I'm sure that everyone remembers those **green** Bibles that every Jehovah's Witness had years ago. Keeping up with the speaker as he told us to turn to the scriptures was an experience. If you think that you know your Bible, try going to the Kingdom Hall and finding the scriptures as the speaker give them to you. They used tons of scriptures to support the information. Those minor prophets are still giving me trouble sometimes. Oh, the differences made a nice impact on me. Yet, I continued trying to praise God at church, hoping for a different outcome. Nonetheless, I never felt comfortable at church anymore and changed churches many times. I went to other churches in the areas but I still had that 'empty' feeling. I joined one last church, the one mentioned above with Sister Rogers. It reminded me of eating some of those energy bars that taste like cardboard with peanut butter on top. Eventually, I stopped going to church for the most part...except for funerals and weddings.

Life continued to 'beat me up' as I remarried to someone that had some addiction problems. I tried everything within my power to make a good life but most of the time things were in constant disarray. Going to church seemed to ease the pressure that I felt but I just couldn't see any hope, feel any hope or sense any hope. On the final Sunday that I went to church, I came home with an utter feeling of ***nothingness.*** I can't describe all that was going through my mind except the fact that I felt that there was no one to talk to about what I was feeling that would understand. However, I felt that I had to 'put on a happy face for my daughter'.

I remember that I had been crying my eyes out and the phone rang (there was no caller ID) and I answered it. I heard my oldest brother's voice on the other end sounding happy but 'for the life of me,' I can't remember what he was saying. It all sounded like a hummm… in my ear. Finally, the first distinguishable words were questioning me about my previously studying with the Witnesses. I immediately had somewhat of an attitude, asking him why he was asking me about studying with Jehovah's Witnesses. He told me: "I'm one of Jehovah's Witnesses." My first question was: "Does Mother know?" He said "No." I said: "Oh, she's going to be mad." He said: "I'm trying to serve Jehovah, not Mother." I can remember thinking: "Boy, that's a bold statement, but wait until she finds out." I asked him why did he join and he explained and proceeded to ask if Aunt Gladys was still a witness. I said yes. He then proceeded to tell me that he wanted me to study the Bible again, this time with an open mind. He told me to call Aunt Gladys and ask her to call the person that studied with her and ask them to come and study with me. He was so very excited as then told me that my other brother and sister were studying and learning the truth about God. For the first time in years, I felt a ray of sunshine!! As a result of Jehovah and my brother's concern and love for me, and Jehovah's angel guiding him; my brother got me started in a new direction that I still thank him for today. I started studying and eventually I started to attend some meetings. I always enjoyed the meeting, the people and the information that was always Bible-based.

After experiencing some of the Sunday meetings, I finally went to a district convention in Macon, GA. My daughter, my best friend (at the time), and myself shared a room for three days. That, too, was an experience. There, I was utterly amazed at the number of people that were from all sorts of backgrounds, ethnic groups and races, over 3,000 people. Everyone was hugging each other and smiling. The children were well-behaved and neatly dressed. All in attendance were dressed modestly with no outlandish styles. There was peace and harmony everywhere I looked. At the end of the day, there was no trash all over the floors or the grounds! The bathrooms were cleaned as well. Those in attendance did all the cleaning, sweeping and mopping. I was truly impressed! I felt pressure from family members and others to give up studying and come back to the church. Nonetheless, I stuck with learning and serving Jehovah.

Years later, Jehovah offered me another opportunity to serve Him in truth and I accepted. I studied the Bible for a couple of years and tried to learn basic Bible truths. Afterwards, I made a dedication to Jehovah in prayer; that I would serve Him the very best I could, for the rest of my life. I started sharing the things that I was learning with others and had to "eat my words" about never going out to someone's house - uninvited. Now, I am one of over eight million witnesses worldwide, in over 240 lands, preaching and teaching others about the wonderful promises found in the Bible. I spend up to 40 or 50 hours during certain months going from door to door (Matthew 28:19,20) in obedience to this command. Some months I spend 30 hours out in the ministry if it is a *special* month. It is truly refreshing to find those ones that are truly interested in learning Bible truths and then having some meaningful conversations.

The things that are being taught Worldwide are the same from one congregation to the next, from one country to the next, so all teachings will not vary from person to person or place to place. The teachings are the same, emphasizing the unity of Jehovah's people. There's nothing that can compare to learning what the Bible teaches. The Bible is our only and best source for finding the truth about God, the earth, the heavens and those that are obedient to the word of God. Obedience is better than a sacrifice, so obedience to the truths that we find in the scriptures helps us to draw closer to God and have His blessings.

The Bible begins with the loss of a paradise, offers comfort in these trying times and promises a wonderful outcome for all those who are obedient as well as those who have died and are in God's memory. Psalm 37:9,10 promises that the meek will inherit the earth. Verse 29 says that the righteous will possess the earth and reside forever upon it. Revelation 21:3,4 says death, pain, mourning and tears of sadness will be no more. Isaiah 11:6-9 holds out a wonderful promise as well and as Isaiah 65:17 says the former things (bad things) will not be brought to mind; 21-25 tell us that houses will be built but not for someone else to inhabit. They will plant but not for someone else to eat. And then, something that we will never witness now - a lion and a bull eating straw together or the wolf and the lamb eating together. Jehovah says that there be no ruin in His holy mountain. (His Government). Isaiah 33:24 tells us: "No resident will say, I am sick." Since we are living in critical times as the Bible says, all these promises may be hard to imagine or accept. But the God that cannot lie and can do anything that He desires, will do what He desires...clean up the earth. So, the Lord's Prayer that I have prayed since I was able to talk will have its fulfillment, and soon, all of us will be able to say in unison: "Free at last!!" Free from everything bad!!

"The truth will set you free." John 8:32 helps us to appreciate this truth, "By gaining an accurate knowledge of Bible truth, we are free from God-dishonoring teachings and practices promoted by so many of the world's religions," (Watchtower Bible & Tract Society).

Teachings that promote pagan doctrines bring no praise to God, however, many are content with what they have been taught and are being taught. Some teach that humans have an immortal soul that goes to the spirit realm when the body die. The Bible teaches that when someone die, they go to their grave and await a resurrection (John 5:28,29). When Jesus was with his disciples, he likened death to sleep, indicating that the person was in a sleep-like state and could be resurrected or awaken. He showed this with his resurrection of Lazarus. Some teach that God is to blame for all of man's woes, even insisting that God approved of or caused the person's death - saying 'He needed another flower in His garden' and 'He is too wise to make a mistake.' Statements such as these make God look hateful and greedy. Many churches are now teaching 'prosperity' teachings which are in direct conflict with Bible teachings (1Timothy 6:6-10). I was also amused to learn that tithing was for the Jewish system as a means of support that Jehovah had set up for those that worked at the temple and did not have jobs or a means of support. Once Jesus came to the earth and died, tithing was done away with along with the law. I was grateful to learn that the scriptures tell us at 2 Corinthians 9:7: "Let each one do just as he has resolved in his heart, not grudgingly or under compulsion, for God loves a cheerful giver."

Our Kingdom Hall hosts two different congregations; one English-speaking and one Spanish-speaking. There are some Kingdom Halls that may host up to six or more congregations, some with more languages such as Chinese, Vietnamese or Ethiopian. There are new language groups being formed each month as new ethnic groups begin to move into the United States. Jehovah shows his love in that He makes it possible for every language group to serve Him in truth. Cleaning arrangements are different at each Kingdom Hall as the congregation is divided into groups. Each group is assigned different assignments as the weeks go by. There is a list for

Kingdom Hall cleaning, inside and out, a list for feeding the speaker for the week, a list for the sound system and reading the Watchtower magazines. No one is confused about their duties. The men take the lead, as Jesus said that the head is the man and the head of man is Jesus and the head of Jesus is Jehovah.

Many of us take part in building our Kingdom Halls or in the repairs. Women are trained to do almost any type of work that the men do. There is nothing off limits if the women and children want to learn. The children are taught different skills as they become older and according to their abilities. We look at this training as precursor to the time when God will need all those willing to help cleanse the earth and build suitable housing for everyone.

So now, I can say that I finally know what the truth has set me free from! The truth has set me free from unscriptural practices such as looking for omens and superstitions. I now look forward to a time when the whole earth will be cleansed, wicked people will be removed, and peace and righteousness will reign forever. Think of the time when all those dead will arise and be brought back to perfect health and youthful vigor! No eyeglasses, hearing aids, walking canes or wheelchairs needed here! Running, jumping, leaping and laughing! The new world is here!

Yes, My *brain* has been *washed* clean and I am free!

All Witnesses offer free home Bible studies to anyone that is interested as a part of our ministry and we are willing to do so at their convenience. As part of my ministry, I also write letters to those that I cannot reach at home. Sometimes I also make phone calls to those that I am unable to reach. There are some that like to so their study over the phone and over the computer. It's really left up to the individual and what is best for them.

We have a wonderful website, **JW.Org,** available in over 720 languages that consists of talks, videos for families, children and teenagers. There are life stories of some who have found that Jehovah's mercy extends to anyone who wants to repent and turn around. There is news about what is going on around the world. There are reports about the court case that Russia had against Jehovah's Witnesses and how they unlawfully seized their properties. You can read about how donations are being used, how literature is being distributed and how the missionaries learn new languages and live in their respective communities. You can see videos that show how the literature is delivered in places like the Congo, Myanmar, and other hard-to-reach communities. **JW.Org** provides a wonderful assortment of spiritual meals served from the best hosts ever, Jehovah God and his son, Jesus Christ.

May all honor and glory go to Jehovah, the Grand Creator of all things.

The Ministries of Helps

Demetria Hill Cannady, PhD, LPC

Over the course of a few months one of our ministers, LaTronza Sanford, conducted a Bible study on the Ministries of Helps using the book, *The Ministry of Helps,* by Dr. Buddy Bell. The study was informative and thought provoking. Within this study, she made us aware that "helps" is a calling; an anointing. She also defined H.E.L.P.S. for us as Having Enough Loving People Serving. To minister is to contribute; to serve; to attend; or to wait upon. While the key focus was the ministries within the church it also applied to the ministries outside the church. Each individual participating in this book project has a "helping" ministry inside and/or outside the church. The heart's intent is a component of the ministries of help- Is your heart pure when you do something for someone, even the unimportant things which may seem insignificant to us.

Minister Sanford shared, "As servants, inside and outside the church we encounter individuals that have "soul wounds" which are caused by sin and trauma most often in our childhood. Some of these soul wounds come in the form of hurt, disappointment, molestation, abuse, and abandonment most often by the vows who vowed to protect us." These "soul wounds" are dangerous because they can't be seen but we may carry them around in our hearts for decades and sometimes pass them on to the next generation. She continued, "If unhealed they continue to fester thus turning into long-lasting anger, resentment, bitterness, hatred, and unforgiveness. Unforgiveness is noted to be the biggest soul wound." When we encounter these hurting individuals, we, as helping professionals must know how to assist in the helping of these soul wounds. We must assist individuals in word and in deed. God places gifts in us that we need to complete the assignments that he has given to us. To assist we must be knowledgeable within our craft (gifts) and be able to receive ongoing training due to the changing times. "Knowledge eliminates fear and training is important," as stated by Minister Sanford.

I can tell you that I have been in the helping field for a long time but I never viewed what I did as a ministry until the Bible study on the ministry of help was conducted. My spirit felt convicted in so many ways, primarily because I have a habit of cutting people off. If they wrong me, I was done associating with them outside of speaking. Now, after hearing and processing the study on the ministries of helps- I can and will get weary but I'm not allowed to quit. This continues to stick with me even though this Bible study has ended. When you are deemed a servant, you must continue to serve even in the uncomfortable places.

As you continue to journey with each contributing author, you will also take a journey through tidbits and information about mental health, mental well-being, and spirituality as it relates to individuals with mental health topics. Believe it or not, most individuals that have "church hurt" and/or leave the church has a form of mental health issue. Mental health does not mean that you're crazy, it just means that your thought processes are functioning well or not so much. We have good mental health and well-being and then we have those who have neglected to take care of their mental health by the fear of being stigmatized. In the black community when we hear mental health we automatically assume someone is "crazy," which may be farther from the truth, especially if you practice good mental health (therapy and/or prescription medication, as prescribed). Many view seeing a therapist as a sign of weakness. During the "old days," children were often reminded that "what happens in this house stays in this house" so there wasn't a recourse but to keep family secrets even if the secrets involved you.

There are 13.2% or 45.7 million people in the United Stated which identify as Black or African American. Of those who identify as Black or African American over sixteen percent had a diagnosable mental illness in 2014. That equates to over 6.8 million people who were diagnosed with a mental illness (U.S. Census Bureau, 2014). There are many events which happen to us and through the course of genetic predisposition which can cause us to have a mental illness. Events in our lives which can cause us to have mental health issues may present in the form of trauma such as: addiction (drug and alcohol) by the individual and/or immediate family member, molestation, rape, sexual abuse, death of a parent, family member, and/or child, seeing someone get killed. Most incidents such as these are referred to as incidents which can cause Post Traumatic Stress Disorder (PTSD) because you relive the trauma long after the incident has ended.

With the genetic predisposition, someone in your family lineage may have suffered from a mental health diagnoses, treated and untreated, which means that the genetics are passed down from generation to generation. You may not have a mental health disorder because your parents or grandparents did but your children can have a mental health disorder. Genetics can and will sometimes skip a generation.

Post-Traumatic Stress Disorder

Demetria Hill Cannady, PhD, LPC

Post-Traumatic Stress Disorder (PTSD) is the exposure to actual or threatened death, serious injury, or sexual violation. The exposure must result from one or more scenarios in which the individual: directly experiences the traumatic even; witnesses the traumatic event in person; learns that the traumatic event occurred to a close family member or close friend (the actual or threatened death being either violent or accidental); or experiences first-hand repeated or extreme exposure to aversive details of the traumatic event (not through media, pictures, television or movies unless work-related) (American Psychiatric Association, 2013). PTSD is commonly associated with veterans. However, veterans are not the only individuals which experience PTSD as you can see from the description of PTSD.

Individuals who experience PTSD can have events (the traumatic event) which replay over and over in their minds. The replaying of these events often cause distress, flashbacks, and may impair the individual's ability to function personally, socially, or on their jobs. According to the DSM-V there are normally four (4) behavioral symptoms which accompany PTSD: intrusion, avoidance, negative cognitions and moods, and alterations in arousal and reactivity. The intrusion may manifest in nightmares, flashbacks, and/ or intense or extended exposure to the traumatic event. Avoidance can manifest in thoughts and feelings along with reminders such as people, places, conversations, activities, objects, or situations (American Psychiatric Association).

Negative cognitions and moods will increase or worsen through continuous negative beliefs about the situation, blaming self or others, dissociative amnesia (not due to head injury, alcohol, or drugs), persistent trauma-related emotions (fear, horror, anger, guilt, and/or shame), decrease in activities that the person used to enjoy, and withdrawing themselves from family and friends (American Psychiatric Association, 2013). Alterations in arousal and reactivity will worsen by the individual becoming more irritable or aggressive, hyper-vigilant, self-destructive or reckless (promiscuity and/or alcohol or drug use), problems concentrating, easy to startle, and experience problems with sleeping (American Psychiatric Association).

Many African American women experience the self-destructive behaviors after a traumatic event such as molestation or rape; these individuals will engage in promiscuous behaviors, some in part because they think this is "normal" behavior to allow another individual to have control of their bodies. Others indulge in alcohol and drug use to block out the recurring memories or pictures of the events. This works momentarily until the individual becomes sober or the drugs "wear off" thus bringing them back to the empty feeling they previously were having.

American Psychiatric Association (2013). Diagnostic and statistical manual of mental disorders, 5th Ed. Washington, DC.

 Tonya Davis-Taylor, LMSW, FDLC, is the Founder and CEO Transform-Simply by Doing, LLC where her goal is to assist Women of Color on their transformational journey. Ultimately, she is here to support Women of Color increase their sustainability, build leadership capacity and to foster a network of interdependence with other women of color leaders. She is a licensed Master Social Worker, manager, career & executive coach, trainer and consultant with a private practice in New York City. Tonya is a thought leader in the social services industry and agent for Transformational Leadership. She has more than 20 years of experience helping individuals, couples, and non-profit organizations.

Tonya received her Master Degree from Fordham University Graduate School for Social Service with a concentration in research and a Specialization in Children and Family Services. She also holds a Bachelors' of Science in Criminal Justice from John Jay College of Criminal Justice. Most recently, Tonya completed IGNITE Fellowship for Women of Color in the Social Sector and Stand in your Power Transformational Leadership Program ¬ Tonya is the recipient of numerous academic awards and honors including the ACS leadership Development Scholarship, Ronald E. McNair Scholarship as well as the Thurgood Marshal Scholarship.

Tonya's passion is people. Her desire is to inspire all her clients to achieve their personal best; to begin to change the dynamic of their stories to not only include the hurt, trauma, and suffering, but their triumph of healing, hope, and reconciliation. Tonya lives in NYC with her two children.

Tonya is currently writing her first book "Transform, Simply by Doing- Nothing New Just My Perspective" For more information, please contact her webpage.

Contact Information:

Transformsimplybydoing@gmail.com
(718) 288-5437 Phone

You Can't Heal What You Don't Reveal...

TONYA DAVIS-TAYLOR, LMSW, FDLC

It all happened in 1986—my first test with faith. Surely, I would have passed the test as I've spent my whole life in the church. I mean that was the longest sixteen years of my life. I was attending Sunday Service all day literally; Sunday school, the 8am, the 11 am services, and you can't forget Young People Willing Workers (YPWW) in the evening. I had to be prepared for whatever was thrown my way. There is no way I wouldn't be equipped for whatever the devil had in store for me. After all I had been taught to pray and have the faith of a mustard seed and God would see you through.

If you will go back with to the eighties, what started out as the best times of my life abruptly ended into what I thought then was the worst time of my life. I know now it was the most transformational time of my life but it has taken me a lifetime to appreciate it as such. I remember the birth of hip hop, the Cosby Show aired on primetime TV, The Color Purple was written, and Oprah was trending before trending was a thing. I also started to really come into my own as I started high school in the mid-eighties. I was truly an "around the way girl," with at least two pair of bamboo earrings.

With all the good that was going on there were two things that happen during this same time frame that was detrimental not only to my family to many other African American families. There was the increase in opiates use (back then it was simply heroin) and this new disease called Auto Immune Deficiency Syndrome (AIDS). Both would cause irreparable damage to so many families. Many families to this very day have gaps in their linage due to this solemn period, which predated the crack epidemic which we all know was catastrophic to the African American family.

In my naiveté, I had no idea that both would change the course of my life forever and be my biggest test of faith as well my life work and personal mission. In the height of the AIDS epidemic, it was all over the news, if you got it, you died a horrific death- quick but a complete breakdown of your body. Initially, the news reported that AIDS was impacting gay men for the most part. It was an ugly disease and showed no mercy to those who contracted it in the eighties.

I was a teenager, so in classic teenage form I couldn't rationalize that this would impact me and test my faith. Here's the thing I didn't have any idea if, how, or why I would be impacted by either the heroin or AIDS. I'm certain that I didn't even have the language to describe what was about to happen to my brothers and me. What I do know that my family never discussed my mother's illness or her battle with addiction.

My family, no different than many other families definitely had a cloak of secrecy on anything deemed dark or ungodly. There were many things that stayed within the family and many others that knew but never talked about. I remember growing up and seeing my parents do drugs but I knew never to ask or talk about it. I knew my mother had because I read the chart that clearly said HIV+. I grew up pre-Google so there wasn't a way for me to check anything that I thought I knew, so most of my information came from the news. I remember asking an aunt, what did that mean and she just looked at me with no response. I was old enough to know at that time, my mother's death was imminent whether they told me or not. The silence was deafening and left me completely vulnerable I remember thinking I would sacrifice anything if God spared her life. He did not!

Proving to be my first fall out with God, I didn't have a full understanding of how faith worked and definitely had not mastered discernment. I believed if I prayed for something, God granted it and all is right with the world. To my dismay it didn't quite work like that and my prayers I felt then went unanswered. I've seen people pray and their prayers were answered so I felt unworthy and that in some way my mother and I were not worth saving. I was left to navigate my own feelings of loss, growing up motherless, and knowing the non-talk about components of my mother's life. It took many years for me to learn to trust God again, and quite frankly it was not the church that brought me back.

It was many years of psychotherapy that gave me a better understanding that what happened to my mom was not God's personal vendetta against me but the sum of how she lived her life and consequently how she loss it. For years I lived with "survivor's remorse," guilty for being alive, and 18-year-old matriarch trying to use one system to heal when I needed multiple support streams to heal the hurt and began to trust God again.

Trauma is defined as a deeply distressing or disturbing experience. Emotional and psychological trauma can be caused by single incident- one-time events or a series of events that have a negative impact on a person, such as a horrible accident, a natural disaster, or a violent attack or unforeseen death. It can leave you with uncertainty, anxiety, and fear.

Emotional and psychological symptoms of trauma:

- Shock, denial, or disbelief
- Anger, irritability, mood swings
- Guilt, shame, self-blame
- Feeling sad or hopeless
- Confusion, difficulty concentrating
- Anxiety and fear
- Withdrawing from others
- Feeling disconnected or numb

Physical symptoms of trauma:

- Insomnia or nightmares
- Being startled easily
- Racing heartbeat
- Aches and pains
- Fatigue
- Difficulty concentrating
- Edginess and agitation
- Muscle tension

Fast forward to 2016, life has taking me through various up and downs. I'm not who I was 30 years before. I've learned to lot. I know how to manage my feelings. I'm super at self-care, after all, I facilitate workshops on it. This next plot twist through me a loop and after a year worth of processing, I became that same scared little girl I was in 1986 just wanting to live. After having surgery and visiting my surgeon to get my release to return to work, I noticed the look of concern on his face. I thought it was interesting since it was a beautiful day out, I was going back to work, and I was ready for this new beginning and clean bill of health. He said a lot or not so much I cannot remember. I thought I was in Peanuts episode and he was a teacher, "womp womp womp." A lot of talking about nothing-or maybe it was something, I really do not remember. I caught the last bit of what he said or at least I thought I did—Cancer!

He was looking at my chart but could he be talking about someone else and he has mistaken me for another patient. He must have gotten me mixed up with someone else but he insisted that I call an oncologist before leaving his office as this wasn't his expertise. Talking about the very air you breathe being snatched from you. I was paralyzed. Things were happening around me but I was stuck. I was 45 years old and somehow, I lived 10 years longer than my mother. I've done things she could only imagine. I've seen more of children accomplishments than she had but will our fate be the same, gone to soon. I know exactly how ugly Cancer can be; I've lived it when it stole the life of my beloved adoptive mother. And here it is again coming for me; like I did not have time for this, for real.

After getting my bearings and an 1st, 2nd and 3rd opinions I realized that I had to face what was deemed mine, Lymphoma (not terminal-thankfully) and I started treatment which I'm still undergoing. The gift with this disease unlike with my mom, it afforded me the 2nd chance to right wrongs, get things in order, and love on those that I love and to be loved on. Know this, prayer works but so does talking to a mental health professional. My Cancer diagnosis didn't just impact me but those I have impacted; my children and family had to accept this as our new norm.

The one thing that I've learned from both experiences is that my spirituality was just as important as my mental health. My early denial of my diagnosis was not letting me fully deal with my plight. If I had stayed in denial I would have never gotten treatment which had the potential to heal me. You need both. Mental Health wellness is just as important as medical wellness and spiritual wellness. My healing from Cancer was a three-part component. Each was essential to my healing.

I needed my medical doctors, my therapist, and my spirituality to get me through the last year. I'm grateful for my integrated team of healers.

It's been a year and two different treatment regimens and I still live with Cancer to date. Trust me I've been praying, following doctors' orders, and living a healthier lifestyle but still I live with Cancer. The real blessing here is- I still live!!! Some things are beyond our immediate understanding; we just must go through storm trusting that what is supposed to be will be and what is, is.

Moving Forward-Healing Steps:

Going through the healing process does not undo the negative effects, but it will allow the trauma to co-exist with your healed being. I've outlined three phases that are critical to relieving yourself from the burden of the trauma. They are as follow:

Retreat

It is extremely difficult to experience something traumatic and not take the private time you need to process the impact of the traumatic events. One must take the time they need to honor the pain and mourn the loss before they can move on. I would caution not to stay in this phase for very long, as it will not serve you very well to be there longer than necessary. However, it is critical that you honor your feelings. Please remember to honor your feelings; process what has happened; and grieve the loss.

Release

After any traumatic event one most free themselves from the hurt the pain and any feelings of rejections they may have. There are two choices; wallow in self-pity or become the victim or decide to be the victor by releasing the trauma. There is no scientific way or a time frame that one can state how you will move forward or how long it will take to move forward. You just have to do it and it must be purposeful and intentional. These following steps will help you to move forward:

Professional Therapeutic Care -help from a professional to help you process your feelings can be helpful Therapy can be an effective treatment for mental and emotional trauma.

Attitude of Gratitude- If you focus with gratitude on the things that are good, you will find the strength to confront the things you want to change. Be present in the moments. Learn to appreciate the little things.

Positive people- Surround yourself with positive people. Their energy could sustain you. Also remain positive, the universe has a way of returning those positive vibes.

Kindness and compassion- Be gentle, kinder and more loving with yourself while you are healing.

Faith. Prayer or meditation will make all the difference.

Rebuild

Exercise - When so much is out of your control, exercise is one thing you can start *and* finish.

Laugh - Laugh! It will change the chemistry within your body. Watch a funny movie.

Network/Support- Allow yourself to be supported. Learn to lean on your network. Sometimes one has to lean in their power until they are strong enough to stand in it.

Create a New Story- You are the author of your story, and you decide how it will end. Keep showing up for life and define it on your terms. I consciously choose to remain a leader; a leader that needed support but a leader nonetheless.

I tell this story because there is someone who is going through a similar situation. I tell this story because it's my legacy and the generations to come need to know. I tell this story because I come from a woman who was beautiful and strong but was human. I tell this story because it is my story. I tell this story because you can't heal what you don't reveal. Please seek help in any of your unaddressed trauma. It won't go away and often times it manifests itself in negative ways. It's imperative to not rely on one source but to utilize everything at your disposal. Moving past the trauma is a tremendous act of kindness that everyone deserves.

Self-Esteem

Demetria Hill Cannady, PhD, LPC

Self-Esteem is a hot topic among women, especially African American women with the variety of skin tones, facial features, and hair conversations. Self-esteem is our confidence about what we believe about ourselves; our thoughts about our ability, beauty, and skills; it is what we tell ourselves when we talk to ourselves. Self-esteem begins in childhood where we were either built up or torn down regarding our beauty, appearance, body type, size, and stature. When we were children we were impressionable. Some of us were told we were beautiful, talented, and able to do anything that we put our minds to. Others were told that they were ugly, worthless, and would never amount to nothing. Whatever we were told, we believed it whether it was true or not, especially if it played over and over in our minds.

Our peers and the adults in our lives played a significant part of our successes while growing up. Our peers name-called (good and bad) and most often than not, we believed what they said to us. I remember being called "Olive Oyl, "Toothpick," "Skinny," and whatever other names associated with being small-framed. Some would make comments such as, "You're pretty but you're so skinny." I really could have let what my peers said to me take a toll on me but most days I didn't. I used to tell myself often, "You need to gain some weight. You straight up and down with no curves nowhere." Yep, I beat myself up sometimes for being skinny and then other days I reminded myself that when my peers hit their forties- I would be fine as wine!

On the other hand, I had friends/associates that took to heart what was being expressed by our peers. They longed for straight hair, perms, "jerry curls," name-brand clothing and shoes, etc.

so that they could be "a part of." Some used skin-lightening cream while others attempted to tan to get darker. We had shared a piece in the battle of trying to "belong." Luckily, we had adults who poured into us along the way, reminding us of things other than our appearance. We were reminded of our character and academics, which went with the beauty (inside and out). If we had ugly personalities, this made us an ugly person regardless of how beautiful our outer appearance may have been.

There are predominantly two forms of self-esteem; low self-esteem or high self-esteem. I've always been told that there is no happy medium but I beg to differ. Low self-esteem comes to us because we were poorly treated or insulted by someone; parents, family members, peers, or society. This may have stemmed from a person's judgment of us or how we felt we were viewed by people. Low self-esteem is associated by irrational and delusional thoughts and can be experienced by a person who has a physical or medical disability (feelings of being less than). Low self-esteem prevents individuals from being happy, enjoying life, and doing things which they desire to do, especially with relation to living out their dreams because they were told what they "can't do."

When you experience self-esteem, you won't allow others to dictate what you think and feel about yourself, your abilities, nor you dream. You live life on your own terms, sometimes living outside the box. You prove the naysayers wrong. However, some may need assistance in increasing their self-esteem and rediscovering who they are and what they enjoy. There are things which you can do to improve your self-esteem. Come out of you comfort zone or "uncomfort" zone because most people will not do which they are uncomfortable with. The most important to raising your self-esteem is knowing what your wants and needs are; this requires you taking care of yourself **FIRST**. If your weight is a concern which is for most, change your diet, exercise, eat healthier foods, go to the doctor (annually and as necessary), take medications as prescribed, and plan fun activities which you enjoy.

Challenge yourself by buying new comfortable and appropriately sexy clothes and shoes that you may not ordinarily wear. Throw away clothes which make you feel bad or that may have unpleasant memories attached to them. Donate clothes to the Salvation Army, Goodwill, or individuals that you know will benefit from the clothing. Spend time with people who compliment you, make you happy, and make you feel good about who you are and that which you are accomplishing. Make sure your home compliments you with colors which you enjoy, even if you aren't in your dream home. Color schemes can improve your mood and emotions. Make sure your home, whether a one-bedroom or a mansion, is free of clutter and comfortable.

Take the time to learn new skills or hobbies. Do something for others or volunteer, volunteering often makes us feel good especially when we realize that our situations may not be as bad as we think that they are. Most important change your negative thoughts and replace them with positive thoughts daily. Post positive affirmations in your home, work environment, and repeat them daily.

- I am beautiful
- I am kind
- I am rich beyond measure
- I am a leader
- I am smart

- I am capable
- I am confident
- I am strong
- I am healthy

 Dr. Elaine Spencer Lewis is the wife of Johnny Mack Lewis and they reside in Valdosta, Georgia. She is the birth mother of three and the mother of five: Shemekia, Tanjuniki, Tiffany, Erica and Timothy. Dr. Lewis is the grandmother of 11: 6 boys and 5 girls. Dr. Lewis is the oldest daughter of Elder John and Mary Spencer and the late Inez Scott Spencer. She was born and raised in the Holiness Church so her passion for the Word of God has always been first and priority in her life.

Dr. Lewis furthered her education by receiving her Associates Degree in Biblical Studies, Bachelor's Degree of Theology, Master of Arts in Christian Counseling, and Doctorate of Theology. Her desire is to do as commanded in Matthew 28:19-20, "Go therefore and make disciples of all the nations, baptizing them in the name of the Father and of the Son and of the Holy Spirit, teaching them to observe all things that I have command you; and lo, I am with you always, even to the end of the age."

The Steps of a P.K. (Preacher Kid) As Her World Turns

Dr. Elaine Spencer Lewis

The life of a PK…. Yes, I am a daughter of a preacher; born and raised in the Holiness religion; even though I was raised in a Christian home I still struggled. I did not think living a saved life was cool but later in life I found out it was the right thing to do. Struggling with internal battles which come in a wide variety, are common to everyone and stem from our sinful nature, which is very complex and the result of unbiblical thinking. The results of that unbiblical thinking caused me depression, stress, self-pity, emotional instability, and inferiority. Growing up as a preacher's daughter one might think that I didn't sin nor thought about sinning. But, oh how wrong; my struggle started in high school which were the most prominent years of my life. I decided that I wanted to explore the life that others my age was experiencing. During my junior year of high school, I played around with sin and tried to smoke cigarettes, a pack would last me one month. Don't laugh, I said I tried. I tried the wine coolers, tried smoking marijuana, and even started having sex… Preacher's daughter? Yes, the Preacher daughter. Trying to do grown folk's things.

Well I became pregnant with my first child, a beautiful baby girl, she was two months old when her mother graduated from High School. I graduated in 1979 and you would have thought I had learned my lesson but no, still not obeying my biblical teachings- sixteen months later I gave birth to my second baby girl. I got married a few days before she made her grand entrance into this world. The same man was the father of both my girls which was a good thing in this "bad" situation. How many know that the word of God is real? In the book of Proverbs 22:6 it states, "Train up a child in the way he should go and when he is old he will not depart from it."

God began to deal with me through dreams and I started to find the pathway back to my upbringing. In this one dream, I saw the clouds roll back like a scroll and a voice saying, "gather around the time is at hand." People were running trying to hide behind trees and brushes to escape the punishment. Now, I had no idea that this was in the Bible until years later; Revelation 6:14-17 reads, "then the heaven receded like a scroll when it is rolled up, and every mountain and island was removed from its place. Then the kings of the earth and the great men and the rich men and the commanding officers and the strong and everyone slave and free, hid themselves in the caves and in the rocks of the mountains. They said to the mountains and rocks, "fall on us, and hide us from the face of Him who sits on the throne, and from the wrath of the Lamb, for the great day of wrath has come." Who is able to withstand it?

In my dream, I went to take my three daughters to my mother because I knew she was going to heaven and I was going to hell… Keep in mind that in 1982 I only had two children which was during the time of this dream. Well that day I was going to find my ex-husband so we could go to hell together. My third daughter wasn't born until 1985 so therefore the dream stands out and really played a valuable role in my life because of the details within the dream…I never found my ex-husband that day. The dream plagued me for years but in 1986 the revelation came through a co-worker at Levi Strauss. My co-worker told me the reason I didn't find my ex-husband was because God was trying to tell me to seek Him for myself. My heart rejoiced because that was my answer. Everything in my body rejoiced.

I really committed myself to God in June of 1986 after this revelation. Psalms 37:23-27 helps me as I explain to you the steps of a how man/woman are made firm by the Lord; He delights in his way though he falls, he will not be hurled down, for The Lord supports, him/her with His hand. I have been young and now am old yet I have not seen the righteous forsaken, nor their offspring begging for bread. The righteous are gracious and their offspring are a source of blessing. Depart from evil and do well and abide forevermore. I had to take these steps before my battle could be won. I had to clearly see my problem, call it what it is (sin), confess it to God, claim God's cleansing, and counter the sin with God's solution.

Whenever God reminds us what He has already spoken in our lives it sets us up for what He's going to release in our lives. I thank God for keeping His hands on me through all my mistakes. He never left me nor did He forsake me… there were times when I found myself like Shadrach, Meshach, and Abednego in the fiery furnace walking in the fire. I went through verbal, physical, and mental abuse for thirteen years. I almost gave up! I felt as if I couldn't take anymore; my self-esteem was low, self-value was shaken, and depression weighted me down. But one day I came to myself and said, "You don't have to stay in this." It's the devil's job to steal, kill, and destroy. God said, "He came to give life and abundance." I stand here to tell you today that God kept me, He pulled me through the tough times, and He didn't let go of my hand.

I can boldly say God will heal, deliver, and restore you. Just confront your calamity, confront what's bothering you, and confront weakness- what has already failed and seem to not be working. I had to forget about that while I walk through the fire. When I came out the fire not smelling like smoke, I can let you know that "The Lord is Elaine Shepherd;" He makes Elaine lie down in green pastures; He leads Elaine beside still waters. He restores Elaine's soul; He leads Elaine in paths of righteousness for His names sake… Even though Elaine walks through the valley of the shadow of death Elaine will fear no evil; for you are with Elaine; Your rod and your staff, they comfort Elaine. You prepare a table before Elaine in the presence of Elaine's enemies, you anoint Elaine's head with oil; Elaine's cup runs over. Surely goodness and mercy shall follow Elaine all the days of Elaine's life and Elaine will dwell in the house of the Lord forever…God prepared my mind for the Kingdom.

My question to you today is are you Kingdom Minded? What does it mean to be kingdom minded? First of all, I need to determine what the Kingdom of God is. The Kingdom of God is a foundational concept of Christianity because it is the central theme of Jesus's message in the Synoptic Gospels. As a child of God, you are to obey the things that pertain to the Kingdom of God. We must possess the nature of the KING. Who is Christ? We must be in right-standing with the King, which brings me to Matthew 6:10; "Thy Kingdom come, thy will be done in earth, as it is in Heaven. There is a connection between what God does and what we do. God is our Authority. The word authority is the power or right to give orders, make decisions, and enforce obedience. When God gives a command, we are to obey. Being lights of the world and salt of the earth. Our influence is so important because we don't know who is watching our steps but if we allow His Spirit to operate, obey His Justice, and restore order by grace and power to all the disorder that exists in the World.

The Kingdom of God will have a powerful force on evil. After all we are a chosen generation, a royal priesthood, a holy nation, a peculiar people that has been called out of darkness walking into the marvelous light. My whole life changed being kingdom minded, I no longer looked at the cigarettes, wine coolers, marijuana, or sex outside of marriage. I became the Titus 2:3-5 woman that tells us how we are to behave from the oldest to the youngest woman of God. It tells us how to treat our husband, our children, and to be good housekeepers in our home. As women, we have a special assignment on this earth. After all we are God's Secret. Think about it, all we know is God put Adam to sleep performed the first surgery; took out a rib and walked away. He made sure every part was in its place from the twins to the toes, brought us back to Adam, and we became the apple of his eye. WOW Man…so whether black, white, or brown our character plays a significant role in our walk with God. We are not born a woman, a woman we became and that's why we must be confident as we remember that God says we are fearfully and wonderfully made. Yes, it's a man job to respect the woman but it's the woman job to give him something to RESPECT!

As a child, I had to change my way of thinking when I thought that being sanctified was not a "Kool" way of living. I didn't care about being picked out to be picked on for Jesus knowing that Romans 12:2 told me to "be not conformed to this world but be ye transform by the renewing of my mind," so it's okay for me to be different because God made me different. Even as a child my sister and aunt would run and hide from me to keep from playing with me. When I got older I understood that I was a unique individual and all through the Bible those that were anointed were different. I embrace my uniqueness; I am fearfully and wonderfully made. I am real with my praise and worship, that's the only way you will receive anything from God. God anointed me to be me so if I don't fit in I am anointed to handle my uniqueness. I leave everything in God's hands because I know eventually I will see God's hands in everything…Amen!

Just when I thought things was going in the right direction tragedy after tragedy began to happen on my mother side of the family. My mother's oldest brother died, one month later my mother died, and six months later my mother's baby brother died. Sad part about these deaths is all of them died before age fifty; forty-eight years old, forty-nine years old, and forty-seven years old. This changed our lives tremendously; three year later my maternal grandmother died from the pain of losing three children. Like Peter and the disciples my faith began on a downward swirl. I became lax and stopped going to Church. I felt that I was saved and saw no need to go to Church. I could worship just fine at home. As I sat and slowly watched my burning flame began to cool, its red glow was fading. I failed the Lord and I saw the flame of love and devotion burn very low within my heart and life. I had backslidden, but thank God, I did not stay there. God sent a neighbor to get me back on track. This neighbor wrote me a letter that pierced my heart so I cried "Lord, please forgive me of my sin; I am sorry for walking away from You and for backsliding on your Word." God has a way of getting your attention, I am so glad that He is married to the backslider. God delivered and restored my life. I want to encourage you today to not think that your sin is so big, or you have sinned so long that you can't be forgiven because this thinking is so wrong. God is faithful; His love is unconditional. Jesus has paid the price all you must do is come boldly to Him confess your sin you will be washed whiter than snow.

Things were going great and suddenly, I found myself shacking in a relationship. I stayed in this sin longer than I should have but thank God, we got married. During that time, I was shacking, I was not comfortable. I cried many of nights because I knew my teaching and this was not right, even though some people have one boyfriend or girlfriend one after another sleeping with them. Some married couples we knew had outside relationships and it didn't appear to bother them. I was faithful to my mate even though we were not married yet but it was still wrong. I talked to my father-in-law about the situation and he kept me in prayer. As, I said we got it right in the sight of God and man.

My father-in-law turned 90 in 2011 and I asked him what he wanted for his birthday. He said I want to have Church for his birthday. I said, "Okay I will do whatever I can to make this happen." Without going into details, we celebrated his birthday on his birthday. Some family members wanted to celebrate on that weekend because of work. He quickly said, "That's not my birthday," so of course that was the end of that story. I mention this because had I not fulfilled his request that year he wouldn't have had the opportunity to have it come true. He told us that was his first birthday celebration having Church on his day. October of 2011 my father-in-law transition from earth to glory. This man was more than a father-in-law he was a father to me. He was the one that God used to preach the Gospel to both my parents and they were saved under his ministry during a tent revival. He was a part of my life all my life. I came along later after my parents were saved and had gotten married. I was born a year and a day after their anniversary. I mentioned this because I had no idea that years later I would be married to his oldest son… but of course God already knew… ha-ha!

On October 22, 2011, the day of my father-in-law homegoing, I was unable to attend. On, October 21, 2011 I was placed in ICU. This is what happened; my sister-in-law and I went to Jacksonville, FL to pick up my niece and nephew for the funeral. We had a great time riding and singing songs. On the way from Jacksonville I stopped at Southside Recreation Center in Valdosta, GA to drop off the key to the building. We made plans to give my aunt, the only one left out of my Mother's immediate family, a gathering. During casual conversation, my aunt mentioned that she wanted all her sister and brother's children to gather so she can see them all before she left this earth. Being the oldest niece, I put the wheels in motion. Everybody was at their motel rooms waiting for our big day.

I entered the building at Southside Recreation Center and the guy was cleaning the floor. I remember the smell not agreeing with me so I sat in a chair. According to my cousins, they said I lost consciousness. As I was regaining consciousness I could hear one of my cousin saying, "It isn't time for crying, pray, cry later." I chuckle in my spirit as I became fully conscious. One cousin said that she heard the ambulance coming and I said, "Who they are coming for?" They said, "You." I have always had a fear of anything with a siren; fire truck, police, or ambulance. As a little girl, I would go to the first house that I saw with a door open… Ha-ha! They would laugh at me; it's funny now but back then it wasn't.

Back to that night when the paramedics came to check my vitals; everything checked out and they were about to leave. The same cousin that said, "Pray now, cry later," told the paramedics that they needed to see if I could walk before they could leave. We got up and OMG; water gushed out like my water broke. The paramedics told me, "Don't worry about that. Let's walk," so we started to walk and by the time we got to the hallway I felt myself getting ready to faint. I told the paramedics but by the time I said it the second time I lost consciousness again. My children said I was blue all my vital signs were low. I had to take "that" ride in the ambulance. We got to the emergency room and I had a CT scan which revealed that I had threw a blood clot in my lungs.

The first time I lost consciousness I threw a blood clot and the second time I lost consciousness I threw another clot. Me not knowing how serious this was I pleaded with the doctor to let me go home and I come back the next day. The doctor said, "Are you crazy? A lady came in here with the same thing you got last week and died." Of course, this took the fight out of me I yield to my hospital stay. I mentioned this because there was an assignment I had to complete. Remember earlier I mentioned my mother was 49 years old and her brothers were 48 and 47 years old when they died? Well at that time I was 49 years old, a generation curse had to be broken. That night as I entered the Intensive Care Unit they wouldn't let my family come with me because there were about fifty of them. The hospital staff could not believe that all those people were there for one person.

I went into ICU and had a talk with my Heavenly Father. I pleaded the blood of Jesus, he dispatched angels around my room and told Satan his assignment was over. It stopped in 1992 with Inez Scott Spencer. I shall live and not die to declare the work of the Lord. About 3 o'clock, the Doctor came into that room and said, "I know what your chart is saying but looking at you none of the signs are there that's usually there with a person that has a blood clot," (pulmonary embolism) the scientific name. I was hooked up to oxygen when the doctor came in the room and said, "I'm going to turn this oxygen down some." The next morning, they came back and took the oxygen tube off completely… Glory to God!! I had to stay in the ICU for five days. Later they said, "You will step down to the five east." I told them, "No I want to go to five west." They asked, "Why?" I replied, "Because the next step will be me going home." Five days later I made it home. God is so good!!

I mentioned this because no matter what your situation is you must stay focused. Keep your mind on the word of God, pray, and keep the faith. Distractions will come and we do not choose how the distractions will come. The main thing is you don't get trapped in those distractions. We must stir up our gifts and keep growing. I believe that many Christians are missing out on so many of the blessings that they are praying for because they refuse to grow. Many of us abandon our roles in our Christian relationship and we sit back and wait on God to do everything in our lives. Well, can I be honest? There are some things that God just won't do because He has given us the ability to do for ourselves. Instead of sitting and waiting we must cultivate the gifts, talents, and abilities that God has bestowed on our life.

I went back to school after my father-in-law predicted that I would receive my doctorate degree. When he said it, I said, "Okay," but in my mind, I said, "I don't know how this is going to happen" but it did I went back to school. I received an Associate's Degree in Biblical Studies, Bachelor's Degree in Theology, Master's Degree in Christian Counseling, and a Doctorate Degree in Theology. Praise God I accomplished my goal. I dedicated my last year of school to my father-in-law for seeing and believing in me before my steps ever started with me continuing my education.

While on my journey of writing this chapter I became ill again, my legs and feet began to swell. There was so much fluid that my veins were attacked which made it uncomfortable to walk and put pressure on my knees all of which caused my blood pressure to rise. My mind was saying, "Here we go with more pills." I began to tell God, "I don't want to be on these pills," but how many of you know that God is the healer? The pills are not the healer, it's just an earthly thing used but our ultimate healer is Jesus...Jehovah Rapha. As I complete this story of the journey of my steps as a preacher kid; I still have faith in God. I am fearfully and wonderfully made. I am the apple of God's eye. I am a part of the Royal Priesthood. I have been brought with a prize, the precious Blood of Jesus saved my soul, and made me whole. I am a baptized believer, filled with the Holy Ghost and fire. God walks with me, God talks with me, and tells me I am His own.

My age of 55 years old which represents Grace Blessing. II Corinthians 12:9 tells me, "My grace is sufficient for you, for my power is made perfect in weakness." Ephesians 4:7 states, "But to each one of us grace has been given as Christ apportioned it. For it is by grace you have been saved, through faith and this is not from yourselves it is the gift of God," Ephesians 2:8. One last scripture, I want to leave with you James 4:6, "But, he gives us more grace." That is why scripture says, "God opposes the proud but shows favor to the humble."

Father, In the Name of Jesus Christ help us to remain humble and cleanse us, every layer of our soul as a living sacrifice, holy, and acceptable. We believe in the Blood of Jesus Christ, and apply His Blood to every layer of our soul. My mind, reason, conscience, emotion, imagination, will, choice, and all parts of my memory cleanse us of the dark wounds of our mind take back the possession of our mind. May the Glory light of Christ Jesus fill my soul and mind right now to the full binding up and casting out everything planted in my soul and mind and sending it to where Jesus Christ would send it Now...back to the pit of hell!! We receive new life in my soul and every layer of my mind and what I have loosed from my soul/mind and casted out cannot come back another time. I am cleansed by the blood, forgiven by the blood, and sanctified by the blood of Jesus Christ In Jesus Christ Name I pray Amen. This prayer was included because I have been attacked with panic attacks for the last few months and had to be prescribed medication. Someone may be going through this same attack and I did not want to conclude this assignment without sharing this prayer and test!!! By the Grace of God, I am getting better each day!!! Thank You Elohim

Methodology of Christian Counseling

Dr. Elaine Spencer Lewis

Christian counseling is by definition, a revelation of the life and love of Jesus Christ in helping someone change for the better. To reach this revelation we must rely on the Bible and the Holy Spirit to reach our goals and face challenges when counseling.

At times with all of lives ups and downs, life can feel like a roller coaster. We need to seek counseling. Just to deal with coping with everyday stresses and adjusting to these road blocks.

There are five multiple definitions encompass with the word "counseling" such as

1. The offering of advice and encouragement
2. The sharing of wisdom and skills
3. Helping to set goals
4. Resolving conflict
5. Helping to create new paths

The difference between Christian Counseling vs Secular Counseling; The Christian Counselor tool for counseling is the Word of God which is the absolute standard as biblical Counselors. II Timothy 3: 16-17 says, "All scripture is God-breathed and is useful for teaching, rebuking, correcting and training in righteousness, so that the man of God may be thoroughly equipped for every good work." As counselor's you must see the Bible as your source of all truth. The Secular Counselor has no such standard, so they use the latest psychological findings or societal norm, which change with the winds of time. God's Word the Bible change not it's the same today, yesterday and forever more. Christian Counseling and Secular Counseling share the same desire to help people overcome their problems, finding meaning and joy in life and become healthy and well-adjusted individuals, both mentally and emotionally. However, the Secular Counselor have no religious or spiritual basis. They counsel based on worldly things or should I say the world's way of doing things.

As Christian counselors, Christ is the ultimate hope for anyone needing counseling. As counselors, we should offer hope and encouragement through the Bible and prayer. Counselors should be sensitive to where people are in their spiritual walk and to not try to force Christianity upon them but seek to explore their faith resources and enable them to be use for their recovery.

A Christian Counselor's major strategy is to help their clients substitute biblical truth for error as the go about their daily lives. The Counselor knows the truth when it is known, believed, and obeyed are the three important things that are true in setting people free. John 8:32 says, "then you will know the truth, and the truth will set you free." When people are set free, they fulfill their true calling once free one must be restored.

Restoration means to restore; that is putting something back together that has been broken. The command in the word of God is very clear that we "restore" any brother or sisters when God conveniently places them in our path. Galatian 6:1 gives us the command to restore another. The example to describe what restore means is the fisherman and the physicians when they described the mending of the fishnets and the setting of fractures. They both called their work "restoration." The value of a torn net is useless if you cannot catch fish; likewise, broken bones are useless until they are set back in place. Both the nets and bones have to be restored to their former use. The question we must ask our counselee is, how have his/her problems taken them from following the will of God. The ultimate goal of all restoration is to glorify God. One must rely on God no matter what the situation is once their heart and mind is focus restoration begins. My other grandson Tyson was riding a scooter when two girls on the playground pushed him off causing him to fall and brake his femur bone in his right thigh Tyson had to be placed on the stretcher with weight to pull the bone back in place then cast with a body cast. I had another grandson, Caleb, who he fell out of a tree and broke his elbow the physician had to put his left arm in a cast until the bone mended back together. Both situation required the grandsons to undergo the restoration process.

We counsel not to punish, nor to gloat over the persons, or to know their sin only to restore. It is the counselor's desire to bring the counselee from uselessness to usefulness and have victory in The Lord. Paul tells us to "put off" (lay aside) certain things, "put on other things" that process is involved with being renewed all of this is needed; to have a full restoration to take its rightful place.

The Christian counseling objective is expressed in two great commandments the first is, "and you shall love the Lord you God with all your heart, and with all your soul, and with your entire strength." The second commandment, "you shall love your neighbor as yourself." The unsaved is excluded from the Life of God because of the darkness of their mind and the hardness of heart, and they have undesirable patterns of moral behavior: sensuality, impurity, and greed.

You have to change what's going on inside; this is what Paul was talking about when he said to lay aside (put off) undesirable patterns of moral behavior which would hinder the process of restoration. The duty as a Christian Counselor is to bring healing, help, hope, encouragement, instruction, and correction to the counselee. It's hard for one to trust so counseling should always take place behind a closed door and the practice of confidentially is a must. What was shared in the closed room stays behind those closed doors.

Effective Counseling

Effective counseling is a two-way street. It takes a cooperative effort by both the counselee receiving counseling and the counselor. It takes a commitment to make difficult changes in behavior or thinking patterns right. It's important to establish a good relationship to allow the counselee to be completely honest about their thoughts and feelings. An effective counselor can help pinpoint obstacles that stand in the way of the counselee. Usually the counselor will suggest behavioral change that's needed to overcome these obstacles.

An effective counselor can identify negative thinking patterns that might be feeding into the counselee problem such as sadness, depression or anxiety. As Christian counselors, we encourage the counselee to build upon their personal strengths and develop a more positive attitude. Making a positive change takes recognizing the behavior that might have contribute to the stumbling block that had cause the problem from the beginning.

There are **eleven** grounds for effective counsel: **First**, effective counseling is to be <u>Jesus-Centered</u>. Furthermore, the life, death, burial, resurrection and ascension of Jesus must be the grounds for counsel, His life is our example. His death is our victory over sin. A counselor's only hope in counseling is for the Spirit to intervene in life of the Counselee, when the Spirit of God intervenes, miracles occur and God changes our lives. **Second**, effective counseling is to <u>be scriptural</u>; Paul tells us that the Word is the basic for doctrine, for reproof, for correction, and for instructions in right living. II Timothy 3:16 tells us that All scripture is God-breathed. **Third**, effective counseling is to be spiritually inspired. Wisdom is the ability to see from God's perspective. But you must communicate what God wants communicated. Therefore, you must be filled with the Holy Spirit.

Fourth, effective counseling should be discerning. The Christian Counselor may need to bind evil spirits, tear down strong holds and cast out the spirits. It's important to know what spirit is in operation. **Fifth**, effect counseling should be judged for accuracy. There is no "Lone Rangers" in counseling the enemy knows how and when to attack the lone sheep. Counselor's should be willing to seek counseling themselves if needed. **Sixth**, effective counseling is mature. The result of spiritually mature counsel is that you learn the difference between what is right and what is wrong, repent and receive freedom. **Seventh** effective counseling is progressive, as counselor you should always desire that your counselee makes process. However, when the counselor discovers walls of resistance they may be unable to counsel as they would like until that wall is torn down.

Eighth, effective counseling is to be conviction based. The primary reason that most people need counsel is that they, in some way, have not obeyed God nor been taught to follow the Spirit. One most see the root of sin before they enter the road to recovery. **Ninth**, effective counseling needs to speak the truth in love. Once one receives a clear conscience, he can see clearly to make a stand. The truth should bring conviction and repentance. **Tenth**, effective counseling must be prayer-centered. You must begin your section with prayer. Prayer allows God to bring to surface real issues. You receive healing, deliverance and direction when you pray. **Eleventh**, effective counseling must deal with the whole person (spirit, soul and body) each area is interrelated. John wrote in III John 1:2, "Beloved, I wish above all things that thou mayest prosper and be in health, even as thy soul prospereth.

There are mistakes often made in counseling such as giving advice without listening. Listening is an art, you have to practice being a good listener; one must give full attention to it. Make it your goal to deeply understand the other person. Not just be able to repeat back their words. Listen to emotions and watch the body language. Do not judge the person, truly care, be genuinely concerned; do not react emotionally to what's said; empathize with them, do not preach at the person; by hearing them out does not mean you agree with everything said.

Why do we find it hard to listen? It's simple as A, B, C, D, and E

1. Assumption- listens with an open ear

2. Bias- don't focus on any one thought or emotion that you have

3. Control-Listen with your heart as well as with your ears remembering the importance of relationship. Maintain a relaxed, non-hurried posture that communicates that their agenda is important.

4. Distraction-stay in the moment hanging on to every word. Refrain from planning ahead to what you will say. Maintain eye contact which will communicate that you are with them.

5. Ego-work at respecting and valuing the other person. Learn to love your neighbor as yourself.

Mistake #2 Never show a judgmental or condemning spirit. Show concern for people who have sinned. They should sense that you care, not that you condemn. Identify sin as sin, but replace anger, disgust, and condemnation with sorrow and concern. Remember that your goal is to restore the other person to help him/her change. Mistake #3 Talking too much when people are involved in discussion they are more likely to open up and change vs you giving them a speech. Although mistakes will be made, the counselee overall development is important to the counselor. As counselor's we are not perfect, we are human but we strive to perfect our imperfection.

As counselors, the result is our focus hoping to accomplish personal growth that empowers the counselee to enjoy their life in a positive way that they may build their faith and live a successful life. Mistake#4 Giving worldly advice…As Counselor's you can't go wrong when you reveal what the Bible says. The Word of God is the Truth. When you counsel, you have the opportunity to help others turn to God and learn how to apply the Bible's truths, you can help disciple people and encourage them to grow in the Lord. Make the most of every opportunity!! The Counselee is the one who sets the pace, but you counselor must set the tone by building your skills to be and effective counselor.

How to have the Right APPROACH and Right ATTITUDES in Counseling

The best counselor is one whose personality is balance by the Holy Spirit. A balanced approach in dealing with people is vital to effective counseling. Jesus himself was perfectly balanced in His personality;

1. He was trustworthy in carrying out His Father's will. He would do His task, and nothing would interfere.
2. He was gentle when John laid on His bosom, when He dealt with the woman at the well.
3. He was stern when He turned over the money changers tables and when He rebuked the Pharisees.

What is Quality? "Quality is a perceptual, conditional, and somewhat subjective attribute and may be understood differently by different people." The quality of an honest steward is a right approach in counseling. An honest steward tells the truth with boldness, tells the truth with right motives that is to please God; they also tell the truth with sincerity. The quality of a gentle mother is another right approach; you need this to be effective in ministering God's Word, a gentle mother is not burdensome; a gentle mother shows warm affection; a gentle mother shows sacrificial love, "she is the creature of life, the giver of life, and the giver of abundant love, care and protection. Such are the great qualities of a mother.

The bond between a mother and her child is the only purest love we can ever find in our lifetime. This such quality is needed to have the right counselor/counselee approach. The quality of a concerned father is important to be effective in ministering God's word; a concerned father is godly in his walk; he sets proper examples; a concerned father is serious in his words, he should be balanced with exhortation. This affect the emotion and insistence to affect the will of God. My father gave me the greatest gift anyone could give another person, he believed in me. As counselor's you must exhibit this quality of exhortation and concern to your counselee.

As counselors, we need wisdom to know how to apply God's medicine to those who are spiritually ill. We are called to be spiritual physicians and spiritual workers who must know how to handle the irritable. We must know how to deal with those who rub us the wrong way; those who get under your skin." Knowing that it's the person temperament which we will discuss later in this thesis. As Christian counselors, we need to learn how to help the helpless, to direct the directionless, to encourage the discouraged, to love the unlovable. Knowing that people have diverse needs and those needs must be handled in diverse ways. God has the perfect antidote for this healing. There are sixty-six books in the Bible to help in the healing process.

God's medicine is speaking aloud and meditating on healing scripture. God's Word is medicine to our flesh. The Word itself contains the power to produce what it says, just as when God said, "Let there be light and there was light;" healing scriptures contain within them the capacity to produce healing. When talking about applying God's medicine to those who are spiritually ill, we must know what God prescribes. It basically means to put into the mind, to confront the mind; to correct someone's thinking. Wrong thought patterns results are immoral behavior. What a person thinks reveals what he is (his character) so to confront someone that's spiritually ill we must have courage and boldness to rely on the Word of God to straighten out the unruly behavior.

God prescribes comfort when we must deal with the easily discouraged. We must strengthen the hearts of these individuals, this mental deficiency usually is someone who has a mind and heart filled with worry, fear and discouragement. People get discouraged from adverse circumstances such as financial misfortune, family hardships or physical suffering. The discouraged Christian does not need to be rebuked like those who are deliberately walking disorderly. He needs to be cheered up; softly and tenderly encouraged; stimulated by caring words well-though out words; to continue in the battle; to not give up; to re-focus his eyes on Christ and the promises of God.

Those who are without strength God prescribes support; it simply means to give support to someone by putting your arms around the weak and holding him up. God is not saying to condone sin, we are never to sympathize with sin, but with the struggling sinner, we are not to smear the sin in their face, but we are to lift them up out of it. Hate the sin, but love the sinner and hold that person accountable.

Finally, God prescribes patience in all cases. Patience is how you apply the medicine. It's your attitude in putting on the needed tonic. Remember patient has a long-fused, long-temperament, you will be able to put up with internal heat without blowing your top or losing your cool. Patient toward all is so important; it's the level of endurance one can take before getting out of character; in other word, its being steadfast. These are some facts that will help you to counsel with the right approach and conveying the right attitude.

Developing a positive mindset; you must change your attitude to change lives. You must choose the way you perceive whatever that's going on as counselor's. Many times, the company we keep can affect our attitudes. As counselor's we should look for good qualities in people, when dealing with other people, such as families and friends; it's easy to see their imperfections. It is by focusing on people's good qualities that we can make progress. These qualities make you stronger and more powerful as counselor's.

Having the right approach and right attitude in counseling are important steps in successful counseling. The counselor must attempt to help the counselee meet their needs while keeping in mind the needs of others. In essence, the counselor tries to help the counselee understand the need behind the behavior and figure out a more quality way to meet that need. A counselee should be walked through the problem-solving process so that they understand how their emotions, needs, and behavior are all linked to present a positive outcome. The counselor's goal is to help the counselee find solutions. Their faithfulness to God will bring them through all struggles and to avoid pitfalls by keeping scriptures in mind and pray, "Lord, keep my heart focused on the scriptures and trusting your promises to help me always speak Words of unconditional love and respect".

Basic for Nouthetic Counseling

What is counseling? Counseling is that process by which one Christian restores another to a place of usefulness to Christ in His Church. In the Word of God, it is a very clear command to "restore" any brother or sister. The ultimate goal of all restoration is to glorify God. This goal ought to guide one's method, attitudes and activities in helping the counselee. We counsel not to punish, to gloat over the persons or to know their sin. We as counselor's desire to bring the counselee to usefulness and have victory in the Lord.

Nouthetic meaning is Biblical Counseling which suggests that there is something wrong with the person who is to be confronted and God desires the change. Personality and behavioral change helps ones to conform to the image of Christ. In Biblical counseling, there ought to be the aim of preventive counseling if teaching and preaching is applied. There may be many problems the people face that could be alleviated in the first place. In Nouthetic counseling the counselor must meet the person where they are. Pointing out what is wrong and helping them obtain the desirable personality and behavioral change based upon scripture.

It is important as a counselor to get as much information as possible near the beginning of the counseling relationship to avoid drawing inaccurate conclusions. Safety and trust is a crucial step that must be established. Nouthetic counseling is always Biblical counseling in II Timothy 3:16, 17; it states the ultimate purpose of the Word of God in the life of every Christian not only is the Word of God given to make us wise unto salvation and to be the instrument God uses, but it also brings about sanctification in our lives. As experience counselors, the counselor listens to situation and help the counselee understand what God desires and walk patiently with the counselee as they make process in living their life according to God's Word. By using the Bible, it helps the journey of the counselee to turn towards reconciliation and spiritual renewal.

Some General Principles and Practices in Counseling

As counselor's you must act professionally and maintain the highest standards. Integrity is so important being honest, fair, being consistent in word and deed. As counselor's you must have competence, we must possess knowledge, have adaptability, have genuine concern and insight. As counselor's we must work at having the Biblical qualifications fulfilled in our daily lives. The Bible is the textbook for counseling II Peter 1:3 for it tells the believer how to relate to God and man. Confidentiality is a must as counselor's you must respect the counselee's privacy. Handle the counselee's information with due diligence. Avoid those pillow talks to maintain confidentiality.

Keep yourselves counselors from being bias and non-judgmental. Do not judge the person, do not emotionally react to what is said, nor should you preach at the person. As counselor's we must show fairness and be objective, non-discriminatory regarding age, gender, race, creed, national origin, sexual orientation, social position or financial status. We must be a good listener. Don't interrupt hear the counselee out; listen with your ears. Don't gaze elsewhere or interrupt the counselee. We must study to be a good listener. Listen for feelings, facts, overtones, undertones, hidden meanings, etc… God gave us two ears and one mouth so this lets us know that listening is more important than talking. Listening is the process that links the counselor and the counselee; the receiver and the sender in the counseling process.

Effective listening helps build a closer relationship between the counselor and the counselee, allowing them to work together successfully. In counseling situations, you will want to watch those nonverbal gestures and react with empathy, as well as compassion. Counselee may feel nervous, discouraged, humiliated or have other strong holds that are not verbally expressed. Therefore, be aware of what may be happening under the surface as people speak. Watch for the nonverbal body language, facial expressions, body movement, gestures and mannerisms they are all forms of communication. We must rely on the power of God, really rely on the working of the Holy Spirit and the power of God through you and through the Word of God. Not just lip service, but expect God to be at work in the counseling session. Anticipate God being at work in the life and be watching for it by faith. Begin and close every session with prayer.

O Lord, grant me to greet the coming day in peace. Help me in all things to rely upon thy holy will. Help me to be a peaceful presence, especially to those who need to sense your presence. In every hour of the day reveal thy will to me. Bless my dealings with all who surround me. Work through me, use me, love them through me, without them seeing me but rather you. Teach me to treat all that comes to me throughout the day with peace of soul, and with the firm conviction that thy will governs all. For you are sovereign and in control of all things. In all my deeds and words guide my thoughts and feelings. In unforeseen events, let me not forget that all are sent by thee. Teach me to act firmly and wisely, without embittering and embarrassing others. Give me strength to bear the fatigue of the coming day and all that it shall bring. Direct my will, teach me to pray continually. May your Word always be present in me that I may not stray from your will, so that you may be honored by my life!! Amen

Forming and Adopting a Biblical Counseling Model

People are motivated by three basic dynamics or controlling factors in their lives.

1. Behaviorally motivated
2. Beliefs and misbeliefs
3. Motivated predominately by their motions

As I set forth counseling models based on these three dynamics or controlling factors which seemingly motivate people when we counsel. Include is the acrostic—PREACH.

P- Physical Aspects Involved as part of P.I.D. (Personal Inventory Data) it is wise to have a questionnaire that would uncover potential problems in this area. As counselor's presenting symptoms and issues and evaluate and affected with the goal of facilitating a sense of well-being. The total person mind, body and soul is involved in healing of the human spirit. You can't change your behavior and not change your emotion.

R- Resources available it is important to find out what resources that's necessary as a team to support ongoing problems. If the person is a drunkard, on drugs, having difficulty with a sinful life-style of whatever kind, he may need to be helped with constant oversight. Some churches have families who are willing to give this kind of support or ongoing aid to a person or family who must have constant oversight. This may need to continue until they are set free from the problem, and during all the time they are in extensive counseling. This kind of help can be indispensable.

E- Emotional factor of having to discuss painful emotions is a reason one avoids seeking counseling. A counselee may be afraid having to experience this painful emotion and afraid to express it to counselor. When one is not open to their emotions they are reluctance to seek counseling. To have the ability to self-disclose to another is central to a person's decision to seek help because to be helped, the person must choose to reveal to another person private feelings, thoughts, and attitudes. This suggest that self-disclosure is an important element in a person's decision to seek help. Most often because of pride the person is controlled by his feeling. The counselee can change emotional responses by "putting on Christ" and being renewed daily by the Word of God.

A-Action or behavior- Directive Counseling, we have stated that nouthetic counseling is Biblical counseling which is directive and confrontational. It consists of verbal counseling in which behavior, attitudes, and beliefs are changed. This is the entire process of counseling. Some counselees are superficially motived, and yet underneath their motivated appearance, they actively defend against changing long-standing patterns of experience and behavior. A key skill in counseling is that of understanding and working with counselee motivation and resistance. Beyond initial motivation, self-motivation for change can become more critical over time as continued behavioral changes require overcoming obstacles. The counselee must know that motivation is an issue not only upon entrance but throughout the counseling process. One must list specific goals in behavioral term changing activity, which means to set straight again. This consists of breaking harmful, sinful habits and seeking to overcome failures and weaknesses. This includes reconciliation, restitution and putting on new patterns of living.

Change is the goal in all Biblical Counseling although we know that change is difficult. Eliminating the problem is not the goal of counseling, helping the person to personal happiness is not the goal to counseling, change that results in conformity to the image of Jesus Christ is the goal. There must be a changing of present patterns from the past. The counselee most plainly in his personality, attitudes and life-style. It takes discipline to bring about behavioral and personality change.

C- Cognitive aspects of Biblical counseling- Recognition of thoughts and effect on the Life. Biblical counseling always includes dealing with both the inner man and the outer man with thoughts and emotions and with words and actions. For a Christian to live a consistent life, his thoughts, emotions, words, and actions must cooperate with the indwelling Holy Spirit. What a person does influences his thoughts and what a person thinks influences what he does. Sinful thoughts can eventually lead to sinful behavior conversely, thoughts often conform to behavior. People may distort scripture to fit their behavior.

In scriptural counseling, inner thoughts and outer works are intertwined. The outer renewal consists of innovative ways of behaving that are consistent with Biblical principles. Change must take place both in the inner life (thoughts) as well as the outer life (or the actions). Though it's so simple, most people don't know how to be positive. Sometimes, they prefer to stay negative, because it is a more familiar state of mind. If you keep thinking the same thoughts day and night, it becomes your reality. This means that if you want your life to be as you want it to be, you must be careful of what you think…so thinking positive is a must.

As you think, so your life becomes. Changing your attitude and expectations, will sooner or later, change your life accordingly. It is your mind that creates the kind of life you live. If you think positively, you will transform your life accordingly. Everything starts from within, from the simplest action, to the greatest achievement. We cannot always control our external circumstances, but we can control our inner world of thoughts, where everything begins. If you are unhappy and negative, you can change the way you feel and think. With a little work and effort, you can change your attitude, expectations, actions, and reactions, and this will lead to more motivation, happiness, and improved life conditions.

Focus on what you want, not on what you don't want. Focus your mind on the good things you already have in your life. This will cause them to increase in your life. Do not fill your mind with thoughts of lack. Think and believe that you already have abundance, success, love and happiness. Learn to feel, think and even act, as if you are already living the life you want. If you can feel, think and act consistently in this way, you will become happier, and will attract new opportunities into your life. God expects change in your thinking; God desires accurate, truthful thinking.

Homework- an aid to help the counselee is one of the most aspects of counseling. It is the exercise of homework that really brings about change. When homework ceases, so does true counseling it ceases. Homework will help uncover some of the basic problems from the past and the present. It will help the counselee to handle the problem that motivated him to seek counsel. Because all problems must be considered important, genuine, and worthy of working on therefore the counselee needs help as well as hope.

Homework may be geared at reeducating therefore the assignments need to be carefully prepared that it will speak to the counselee problems. Counselees need new insights into their problem and need to see the potential for change. Written homework speeds up the counseling, open their minds to problems, and helps them to see the answers according to God's Word. Homework clarifies expectations and force the counselor to be more concrete and more specific, and the counselee to receive far more help. It will take the counselee back over truth, and into new truth. Patterns for change is set by assigning homework and should be expected from the beginning and accompany every session or almost every session.

Homework allows the counselor to deal with problems and set the stage for change. The counselor is the expert who aims to prescribe the Biblical method for change. The counselor monitors the progress and has the potential to spot problems and deal with them as they develop. Homework helps regulate and discipline the counselor's counseling; with weekly assignments, the problem and goals are set before the counselor. It forces him to talk about solutions as well as problems and to bring about change. This will help the counselor to eliminate talking in circles.

Homework provides a starting point for the next session and each session builds upon the other. When there is failure in doing homework questions should be asked; did the counselees not fine the time? What are their priorities? Do they understand the tremendous importance of their homework? As counselors, we must ask ourselves these questions before relating them to the counselee. If we should find that it's a mistake upon the counselor, counselor you should write out the assignment so the counselee totally understands. Have the counselee repeat the assignment back, aloud, and ask if there are questions.

Assignments such as list your sins, seek reconciliation with that offended brother, write out a praise list, and make up a schedule for your life, as a counselor you need to prepare several studies on various problems that people face and have them ready for homework assignments. As counselors, questions should be written out weekly, advise the counselee to attend church and Sunday school as well as begin a devotional life. These steps will lead the Biblical counselor toward a successful counseling section.

Closing

Demetria Hill Cannady, PhD, LPC

As leaders and influential women in our communities me must be cautious and careful of how we carry ourselves when we are assisting people with issues of any sort, spiritual and personal. I recall reading that **LEADERS** are inteLligent, honEst, creAtive, confiDent, drivEn, and couRageous. As leaders, we know and recognize our value and self-worth; respect for ourselves, and will reach out for help from others when we need it. As readers of this book, we pray that everyone who encounters it recognizes their self-worth, as it relates to their mental health, even if you require help pulling it to the surface.

There are seven (7) stories shared within this book which are being used as conversation starters for topics of religion, spirituality, mental health; the correlations between them and intertwining of the most important two, spirituality and mental health. All topics are very broad as there are hundreds of religions, varying views on spirituality, and a host of mental health topics, many of which aren't mentioned in this book. The conversations need to begin and continue to help disseminate the negative connotations related to religion and spirituality and to break the stigma associated with mental health, especially with the African American community.

Some spiritual leaders and advisors are giving out inaccurate information while others give out no information at all, as it relates to mental health and/or mental health education. Some spiritual leaders feel that individuals with mental health issues have "demons" that can be "cast out" while most mental health disorders relate to chemical imbalances within the brain, while others relate to trauma. This inaccurate information in part, is due to lack of knowledge. Some will tell their lay members that God will heal them, "Just keep praying," and "Pray a little harder." This is true; however, part of the healing comes in the format of counseling and medication (in some cases). God gives physicians the knowledge to heal your physical health through diagnosis and through surgery (if necessary) so it is the same with a mental health professional who heals through talk therapy, play therapy, motivational interviewing, hypnotherapy, etc… and medication, if prescribed by the psychiatrist.

Just as you go to the specialist for your physical health issues because this is outside of your primary physician's scope; think of your mental health as being outside of your primary physician and your spiritual leader's scope of practice, unless your spiritual leader has a counseling and/or Christian counseling degree. A pastor's specialty is spiritual health but he must think about one's mental health as well because he/she is responsible for feeding one's spirit even though the processing is up to the individual. It is my opinion that if you deal with a person's spirituality you need to be mindful of their mental health state as well; that way you can refer them to a mental health professional, if necessary. The ultimate responsibility lies on the individual but let them know "it's OK" to seek additional help when necessary versus shunning them or making them feel "less than" for going to talk to a therapist/psychiatrist.

There are several issues which plague the family, especially African American families: self-image, childhood trauma, molestation, poverty, domestic violence, witnessing domestic violence, sexual abuse, and divorce. Some of these family and mental health issues have been carried from one generation to the next, same for religion. People will continue to practice a religion or go to a church because it's the "home" church or the "family" church while their spirit and spiritual health remains unfed. Some go through the motions of "church" so that they can say they attended church on Sunday. In other families, when individuals leave the "home" or "family" church this can and often presents a rift in the family; the family feels betrayed.

There are numerous reasons given as to why people will leave the church: burn out; church hurt; distractions; marriages; divorces; power struggles; lack of a connection; church relocation; new pastor/ spiritual leadership; change in programs (additions and deletions); drama; unresolved conflicts; church cliques; and church size (growth or lack thereof).

Regardless of the reasons people leave, there are still many "flocking" to the church. Research has shown that in the African American community, the church is the first place where people with mental health issues will go. Pastors/Church leaders are deemed "healers" of the spirit so the individual wants their mental health healed even though the leaders aren't adequately equipped to handle mental health issues. Church has been the "go to" place even in slavery. However, African American churches and the term "mental health" presents as contradictory in today's times. There is shame, stigma, and rejection felt by those who have known mental health diagnosis within the church; they're deemed as "crazy" instead of sick and these individuals will suffer in silence instead of reaching out for help. We'd rather not be called "crazy" and "keep people out our business" than reach out for help, this includes those without diagnosed mental health issues as well.

Our people are suffering and dying from depression, anxiety, anger issues, stress, substance abuse, violence, and other mental untreated mental health issues. African Americans struggle with pride and fear; the two intertwined together creates a fear of embarrassment, fear of rejection, fear of the loss of self-respect, and the fear of loss of control, especially seeking help for mental health issues. Also, some feel that they lack faith if they reach out to a mental health professional versus having faith in God that He will heal them. On the other hand, African Americans don't trust the mental health system or therapy because of the stories they're heard about the medications making you like zombies and the "electric shock" treatments. Over the decades there has been an increase in child abuse, substance abuse, suicides among pre-teens girls, and the death rate of black males. With these significant increases in these issues, mental health education in the churches is a priority.

Churches have always been a powerful institution within the African American community dating back to slavery. The churches have been linked to social justice with the African American communities as well. The "healing station," "emotional fitness center," and the "spiritual renewal and restoration" center for mental and emotional hurts. As therapist and spiritual leaders in our communities, we must begin the conversations about mental health and how it is affecting the African American communities. We can be the "change agents" within our local churches by training the church leaders about mental health, what mental health "looks like," and the signs and symptoms of mental health, giving specific information about diagnoses. Therefore, allowing leaders to assist and guide their congregants to the mental health professionals who can heal their minds while they focus on taking care of the spiritual needs.

What's next? Let's start the conversation! How do we do this? We start by sharing our stories, whether the stories be personal or indirect scenarios, or even the stories within this book. This can relax the atmosphere allowing others to realize that it is "OK" to discuss mental health. In these conversations:

- ✓ Church leaders can get to know and support each other through helping congregants with mental health conversations /issues.
- ✓ Examine your personal beliefs about religion, spirituality, and mental health

- ✓ Talk about what mental health means to us; the individual, church, and community
- ✓ Discuss the symptoms/ risk factors of mental health
- ✓ Talk about the mental health challenges affecting the African American families
- ✓ Talk about the mental health challenges affecting the community
- ✓ Talk about the mental health issues and challenges facing our youth
- ✓ Talk about the mental health issues affecting church/ schools
- ✓ Talk about the mental health issues and challenges facing out elderly
- ✓ Discuss alcohol/ substance abuse being a mental health issue within the community
- ✓ Programs which can instituted within the church/community
- ✓ What can you as a spiritual leader do within your church setting; education and programs
- ✓ As a therapist within your church, what programs can you offer

There is a second book to this spirituality and mental health conversation. That book, while continuing to share the journeys will focus on specific mental health issues in the African American community, as this book discussed mental health topics. Please consider purchasing the second book to this series to continue to conversation.

www.ingramcontent.com/pod-product-compliance
Lightning Source LLC
Chambersburg PA
CBHW080508110426
42742CB00017B/3041